Advanced Praise for *A Psychic's Life*

Michael Bodine shares his most fascinating stories as a celebrity psychic. Discover how Michael receives information from the other side, and how he deals with the responsibilities that come with psychic knowledge. Find out what makes the energy of Michael's famous Hollywood clients so unique. Get a first-hand glimpse at what it's like for a psychic to learn the hard lessons from spirit when his ego gets too big for his own good.

A PSYCHIC'S LIFE

WHAT IT'S REALLY LIKE

About the Author

Michael was young when he discovered his psychic abilities. He spent his childhood studying with established psychics and going to "psychic camp" (somewhat reluctantly) to gain a greater understanding of his gifts. Through the loving support of his mother, Mae, he was able to mature in his practice, while staying true to his own creative style.

Michael has been a professional psychic for more than forty years, giving readings, performing ghost bustings, and speaking at events and conventions. His clients range from celebrities like Melanie Griffith and Gary Busey, to financiers and dog walkers.

A PSYCHIC'S LIFE

WHAT IT'S REALLY LIKE

MICHAEL BODINE

Llewellyn Worldwide
Woodbury, Minnesota

FIRST EDITION
First Printing, 2018

Book design by Bob Gaul
Cover design by Shira Atakpu
Editing by Annie Burdick

Llewellyn Publications is a registered trademark of Llewellyn Worldwide Ltd.

Library of Congress Cataloging-in-Publication Data (Pending)
ISBN: 978-0-7387-5866-4

Llewellyn Worldwide Ltd. does not participate in, endorse, or have any authority or responsibility concerning private business transactions between our authors and the public.

All mail addressed to the author is forwarded, but the publisher cannot, unless specifically instructed by the author, give out an address or phone number.

Any internet references contained in this work are current at publication time, but the publisher cannot guarantee that a specific location will continue to be maintained. Please refer to the publisher's website for links to authors' websites and other sources.

Llewellyn Publications
A Division of Llewellyn Worldwide Ltd.
2143 Wooddale Drive
Woodbury, MN 55125-2989
www.llewellyn.com

Printed in the United States of America

CONTENTS

Dedicated to my granddaughter, Noella

INTRODUCTION

This book is about answers: finding them, seeing them, acting on them.

My hope is that when you're done reading it, you'll have a sense of the magic and power that's out there. That you'll know you're exactly where you believe you should be, and you can go exactly where you think you belong.

I hate when people tell me what to do or when they profess to know more about my thinking than I do. So this book isn't about telling you what to do or what to think. These are stories; you make your own conclusions

I just ask that you please have an open mind. Maybe don't just assume I'm trying to con you for fame and fortune. Fortune, maybe, but you can keep the fame.

Even with all the proof, the videos, the testimonials, and the eyewitness accounts, there are still idiots out there who refuse to open their eyes even a little. There's one clown who claims to offer a million dollars for proof that psychics are real.

There's no point in dealing with a person like that. Their fear and insecurities won't allow them even the slightest thought that maybe there's some unseen magic out there. They would rather think themselves insane than have belief. I should know. I was one of those people.

I've struggled for years with all this psychic stuff. Is it real, is my mind playing tricks? How the hell do I really know some of the stuff I know? How did my mom or my sisters know things I never told them about?

I've been on my knees more times than I'd care to admit, begging for some sort of sign or reason why things are the way they are. I understand how it feels to seek guidance. I've been surrounded by psychics most of my life and I've gotten so many readings that I should write a book. (Wait, I *did* write a book.) I've questioned just about everything there is to question about life. People come to me for answers for their lives, and I'm still trying to understand my own.

I've struggled with who I am and why I feel the way I do. Why am I so weird? I say the wrong things and do the wrong things. I never seem to have good balance. Why can't I just be normal? Join a bowling league and shut up?

I often wonder if I'm too out there. Maybe people think I'm an idiot? I know I'll never be voted most popular or greatest guy—I'm odd and awkward. I've literally had my head examined several times since I was a kid. Not the kind where they ask you if you ever killed a family pet (although I have had those too). I mean the kind of examination where they plug a bunch of electrodes into your head, then flash lights and make noises, just to see "what's going on in that weird head of yours."

I've gone to counseling for depression, anxiety, and guilt. I've tried group counseling. I went away for weekend self-esteem camps and power of the mind camps. Physical therapy, emotional therapy, spiritual therapy, even light therapy. I've tried just about everything I could think of, hip or unhip, legit or just stupid, to get an understanding of why I feel the way I do and how to feel better as a person. But whatever answers and solutions I got only seemed to last a week or two and then I'd be right back where I started, wondering "What the hell?"

I've thought about suicide. I've thought, "If I just died, it would all stop." The deep sense of dread, of not knowing. Seeing other people succeed, seeing them happy, more gifted, more intelligent.

I've watched people that I know are assholes advance in the world and be treated with respect. What chip didn't I get?

But I know suicide isn't the answer. In my work, I've come across so many spirits of people who have killed themselves that it's stopped me from making that choice. Seeing their frustration and sadness, their loneliness. And the biggest one: their lack of options. Because once you cut that cord, it's done. You don't get a redo. So I kept going.

But after a while, I stopped asking for help. The silence was almost worse than the depression. Or maybe the depression was caused by the silence? Chicken or egg, who knows—I just stopped.

And then one day, I brought my kids to my mom's so she could watch them while I did some shopping. When I said hello, I noticed that she had her *concerned mother* look on, so I asked her what was wrong. She said she was worried because she saw I had given up. She said she noticed that I had checked out a while ago. She asked if I'd let her do a spread for me, which in our house meant she wanted to do a tarot card reading. I told her I was fine, that I didn't need a reading, and that I was done asking for answers. I was tired of waiting for whatever was *going* to happen.

As I stood there whining, she got up and walked toward the kitchen cabinets. "Keep going," she said. "I'm listening." She took out a glass, filled it with water, and proceeded to throw it in my face. "Honey?" she said. "Sit down. I want to talk to you." I was too busy spitting out water to sit, so she started back to the sink to fill up the glass again. I put my hand up as if to say "uncle!" and told her I would sit.

She seemed disappointed that she couldn't throw another glass of water in my face, but went to the rag drawer and threw me a towel instead.

"Are you possessed?" I asked, wiping my face.

"Shut up!" she said.

Then she reminded me of how I was raised. She brought up all the hard times we went through together and how desperate things had gotten. I told her I remembered those times, but that I was tired of "just surviving and not going further with my life." I always seemed to be in the trenches, so to speak, and was never getting the rewards. Once again, she told me to shut up.

She said one of the main things we learned in those hard times was that the answers do come—maybe not the minute or week you ask for them, but they do come. They come at times when you're looking for them and they come at times when you're not. They come through people or they come through situations. They come in big ways and they come in subtle ways. And then she reminded me of the thing I had forgotten the most. She said, "Remember, Michael, this whole experience is about how you see yourself. If you're down, it's because you see yourself as that person." She reminded me that even though we were desperately poor and uncertain of where would sleep at times, we always knew deep down that we would be okay. And we were. She said, "Spirit teaches us. It's what we believe. We make the choices, we're not victims. We decide, not them."

She then paused for a second and continued, "Stop asking for answers. They get sick of you asking and not believing. Change your thinking. And if you can't do that, at least ask for patience." I seemed to be in short supply of that.

Then her frustration turned to satisfaction. "That was pretty good, wasn't it?" She asked with a tickle in her heart. "The water thing, I mean." I told her I was glad she wasn't drinking coffee, which she thought was funny.

I knew what she was saying, and she was right. It seemed that I had forgotten a lot of the lessons I went through hell to learn, and I knew I didn't want to have to learn them all over again. My mom always surprised me. I think about her every day, though she passed away years ago now.

The truth is, psychics aren't here to give you the answers. We are here to show you that there's a power, a presence out there that you don't always see. Our job is to prove that power exists. If you only concentrate on the psychic, you're not getting it. We decide our destiny. We decide if we are happy or unhappy. Successful or struggling. We are in control, and Spirit is here to help us see that.

My Third Eye Is Bigger Than Your Third Eye

What is the deal with psychics? They're everywhere. They're on the radio, in newspapers, on podcasts, and all over the television! They have shops downtown, uptown, in the sticks, in the burbs. If you live in Jersey they'll come right up to you and tell you about your dead uncle Fred.

Back in the day, psychics were few and far between. The market was untapped. Fewer people believed in psychics, so there were fewer people who wanted readings. But if you wanted to make a name for yourself, it was easier—there were very few of us around.

Now more and more people are waking up. They see the value of psychics and they feel their own abilities. People are much more open to getting a reading.

In the old days, people had the decency to sneak behind buildings or hide in the basement to do a reading. Now it's all so public

I bought shoes the other day and the clerk asked me if I was psychic; he said he recognized me from some event I did and asked if I would be willing to give him a reading. (What I *was* willing to give him was a mint. This poor guy could knock a buzzard off a shit wagon with that breath.)

I couldn't imagine talking to him for an hour face-to-face. But that kind of request never happened when I was young.

Now classes and teachers are everywhere. This means more people want readings, but there are also more psychics doing them.

So, what the hell's going on? Why are so many people interested, aware, and in tune with all this psychic crap? Well, I'll tell you what's going on. My sister, Echo, and people like her have changed the game—that's what.

Echo started teaching psychic development classes forty years ago. And she's damn good at it. She has a calming, understanding nature. When you couple that with her knowledge and her nonjudgmental, motherly approach, it makes her a really effective teacher.

She actually cares about psychics and the psychic community. Which is more than I can say for myself.

She is so effective that a lot of her students not only started doing readings, but they also started teaching people. And then those students started teaching people too and it kept building and building, and now you can't spit without hitting a psychic or someone who's "opening up" psychically.

Do I think that's a bad thing? Well, that depends. On the plus side, it has the scientists, the engineers, and the logical types scratching their heads and looking less logical with every denial.

And it has the religious folks looking like hypocrites and naysayers because it doesn't fit their idea of what God is supposed to be.

And it gives the people with psychic abilities a safe place to practice and express themselves. That's always a good thing in my book.

On the bad side, all the exposure lends itself to frauds and fakes. It also has some people believing psychics have more power than your average person and that psychics have all the answers and wisdom. That, to me, is a bad thing.

What Makes Psychics Tick?

What makes us tick? First, let's be honest: being a psychic is a weird, odd, spooky kind of job that a lot of people look down on. And it's not something people normally seek out to do. You never hear a school guidance counselor say, "Gee, Billy, I think you should forget being a bioengineer, I have a great psychic development class you should look into."

Being a psychic isn't taken that seriously as a real job. When someone says they went to a psychic, most people think, "Wow, you're gullible." Wives don't tell their husbands they've come to see me because they don't want to be looked at as stupid. Guys practically come in disguise so no one will see them coming or going. Psychic work is looked at as an oddity, rather than a job.

Just the name itself seems to signify something other than legitimacy. I've gotten into arguments with people I've known for years who have suggested that being a psychic is just entertainment, telling people what they want to hear.

It *is* getting better, but some psychics still don't even look at it as a job. They see it as a higher purpose, a special calling, a "thing" that separates them from normal people.

But to me it's a job. A weird job? Yes, but still just a job.

So back to the original question: What makes us tick, why do we do it?

We do this job because we have to do it.

The thing is, once you see a ghost, witness accurate reading after reading, and watch the cream cheese actually float across the table unassisted, there's no turning back. Your life is permanently altered.

When you're a psychic, you feel things and hear things—even other people's thoughts—that are sometimes to your own detriment. It's pretty common for me to hear a person's thoughts when I first meet them. Not always deep thoughts or run-on sentences, but words and opinions. It's like hearing a talk radio station, but you can only pick up some of the conversation. The bummer is that it's not always nice thoughts.

I'll also run across people who assume I am picking up on their thoughts. And that can be just as awkward, because they're visibly uncomfortable with me.

What they don't know is that I don't care. I figure everyone has a right to their own thoughts. All the readings I've done have taught me not to judge. I realized early on that everybody has that "other side."

Back when I was young and excited about what I do, a woman came to me for a reading. She was dressed in a business suit, well-groomed and eager to talk about the new ventures she was getting involved in. She announced that she wasn't interested in her personal side; she just wanted to know about business.

I preferred doing business readings because it was more straightforward. Less emotion, more black-and-white. I liked how direct she was and by all accounts it was going to be a fun reading for me.

But as I opened up psychically, all I saw was a large dog, a black and brown Great Dane. I asked her if she recently lost a dog, thinking she might be grieving, but she shook her head no, so I continued to focus on her profession. Still, every time I tried, all I could see was that dog.

Finally, frustrated and confused, I asked her what the deal was with the dog. I was taught not to ask leading questions, but my curiosity got the best of me. Besides, nothing else was coming; there were no words, no explanation, just this dog.

When I asked, she looked down and tears started to come to her eyes. It was clear something was up. I offered to change the subject, because clearly she didn't come to talk about the dog. I wasn't sure I wanted to talk about it either because I wasn't a pet psychic. But instead of replying, she just sat there in silence.

Finally, in a quiet voice she said she had become very close to her pet.

I was a pet lover myself. "So what if she likes her dog? It's not like she's sleeping with it," I thought. But then I started getting images of her and the dog, and they weren't just being pals.

They were showing me that they had become intimate.

Now I really didn't know what to say. I had never seen this before and it was surreal, to say the least. Thoughts were now racing through my head. Maybe I was wrong, maybe I flipped a rod and my imagination was running amok.

She certainly didn't look like the type of person who'd be doing what I thought they might be doing, and if I suggested she was and she wasn't, I'd look like the creep.

My mother's words, "Don't judge," kept coming into my head. Still, I struggled to come to terms with what I was feeling. The images were coming in stronger now and I knew I had to say something. I imagined what my mother would do and it calmed me down.

I took her hand and said, "I think it went further than just being close." And with that, she started crying heavily.

I told her I understood how these things could happen, that I was sure this wasn't her initial intent, that things just got out of hand and how the shame must be unbearable. I said all these things as calmly and with as much love as I could muster, even though inside I was barfing and screaming at the same time.

We talked for over an hour about her relationship with her dog. We talked about the complications it caused with other men, how the dog would get upset when she brought a date home, to the point that it was no longer safe for her to do so. We got so involved with the dog talk that we never got into the business questions she had originally come to discuss.

When she left, her energy was considerably lighter; she seemed unburdened and more at peace. Maybe confessing to someone was all she needed to do, or maybe not being judged and stoned to death for what she had done was the relief she needed. Whatever it was, it helped her. From that day on, I knew I couldn't judge another person for what they had done. I might throw away the couch we sat on, but I wasn't going to judge.

I never saw her again after that, but I wasn't expecting to. I was probably the last person she'd want to see after confessing something like that. Still, it was a major lesson for me. It made listening and picking up on other odd things seem easy.

I've come to understand that we are not in this alone. Money and power are not the reasons we are here. Everything has a reason and every action has a cause. You realize that nobody is better than the next person. And most of all, you realize that *everybody* is here to learn.

We need to share the information and feelings we get from Spirit, because if we don't, we feel nuts! It builds up inside, all this information just sits there, and we need the release. And when we do release it, we feel better and we feel calmer.

So, what makes us tick? The need to share what we feel.

Who Are These Psychics?

That's a damn good question. Of course, everyone is different—individual snowflakes that we are—but we do have common traits that sometimes separate us from the normal folks.

First, just know that most psychics are a little touched—you have to be to do the job. My mom used to tell us that in the old days most of the people in the psych ward were just psychics who didn't know how to deal with being psychic. Her thought was this: Everyone has a gift. Some people are really good with math, some people are creative, some can sing, some can talk binary. And some people just have a natural psychic ability. She contended that because some people just have that ability, Spirit was attracted to them.

But most people were uncomfortable with that idea, and the people around them sure didn't want to go there either. So for the sake of everybody, it was easier to assume you were off your rocker than to think you might have psychic abilities.

I used to wish I had that option. I would have checked myself into some psych ward, taken some pills, stared out the window, and drooled all day. But lucky me, I had an enthusiastic psychic mom.

You have to be a little nutty because you have to be willing to step out from the stigma of being a psychic and allow it to just happen.

Whether you believe in psychics or not, you have to know that with every reading, every psychic puts themself out there. They risk everything—their reputation, their income, their self-worth—just by opening their mouth. You have to be a little off to do that. A lot of us don't advertise; it's all word of mouth. So, if we have a bad day, it could mean our careers.

It does get easier with time and confidence, but I've been doing this for over forty years and I still get a little worried before I do a reading.

Psychics "feel" things—people, animals, trees, and fairies. We moon bathe and we stargaze. We have legitimate conversations with ourselves, out loud.

Some of us talk to rocks. Some of us *sleep* with rocks, and that's a fact. Others hug trees. Literally, we hug trees. We space out and drift away, like we're watching the tide slowly recede.

One day I walked into a bookstore, hoping to find any evidence that my first book still existed, when I saw this young, attractive woman—probably in her early twenties—also looking at books.

She was flanked by two young, hip fellows whose sole purpose was to pose indifferently at anyone who dared to look their way.

Normally I block people out—I have that *Shallow Hal* thing where I don't always see the person's outside, but I do see the inner person, the real one. But by doing this, I sometimes see things I don't care about or judge, like flaws, or fears, or the occasional suicidal thought. So it's easier for me to pretend nobody's there.

But there I was, staring at this young woman. And it wasn't because she was beautiful. I have a daughter the same age, and anyone not named Trump will tell you that when you have a daughter you don't look at young women the same way.

I was staring at her because she had some of the darkest energy I had seen in a long time. I was taken aback by how troubled she must be, and I couldn't for the life of me figure out if I should say something to her or leave it be.

Generally speaking, it's a no-no to do what the old psychics called "ambush readings"—going up, unsolicited, to a stranger and giving them psychic information. I can't tell you how many times I've walked by someone and gotten information on them—often deep, life-altering stuff. And some psychics actually make a living off of ambush readings. But it's considered tacky and egocentric by the old-school psychics, because it becomes more about the person saying it than the information they are giving.

So back to the diva in training in the bookstore. As I was trying to figure out what to do, the three of them started walking toward me. One of her handlers—a guy with the tightest pants I've ever seen on a man—looked at me and rolled his eyes, saying sarcastically, "Take a picture." His friend, who was also dripping in hip, rolled his eyes at me as well as they walked by. When the girl passed, she looked at me with a smirky smile and said with a laugh, "Don't worry, honey, I'm used to it."

I suppose I should have been more aware of my looking at her, but come on, I wasn't ogling. It was more along the lines of a caveman looking at an airplane. And psychics don't just look at people because they have black holes like trauma mama; we see auras, spirits, lights, and all sorts of things around people. It can be downright distracting.

I tried stand-up comedy for about a minute in the '80s, but I got so distracted by all the activity in the audience that I couldn't get through a set. Ghosts were showing up everywhere. They were pointing at people they wanted me to talk to, showing me pictures of possible futures for these people. Showing me warnings, like they wanted me to stop the jokes and warn Ethel she was going to get a DWI.

I could hear people's thoughts: how bad they thought I was, what they wished they were doing instead of watching me. I could hear people thinking about their taxes and lawn fertilizer. I heard one lady wondering if she fed her fish. I wanted to tell everybody to shut up so I could make them laugh, but the only sounds in the room were crickets.

I've had other times when people got the wrong impression from my stare. Sometimes I'll meet someone and their guides will say something funny about them.

It has been my experience that we all have spirit guides around us. Not like dead relatives or friends, but actual guides. These are souls that have been around the block a few times, experienced life, seen things, done things. They come without judgments and without guilt. They are here to support and learn from us, and if we ever need them, we just simply need to ask.

These guides are the people I talk to, the ones who tell me what's what. Sometimes I can see them when I do readings for people, and I can always hear them. They show me pictures, possible futures, and blocks that stop us from achieving those possibilities. They come in all shapes and sizes, and some don't appear to even come from this world. But they try so hard to show us a way, even if we can't see it ourselves. I'll get more into them later.

Back to the story. I once met this rather large, gay football player. Right before I shook his hand, his guides brought up how he always wanted to be a cowboy (guides have a sense of humor too). Something about this huge guy riding a horse struck me as funny, so when I shook his hand, I was smirking. He must have asked me out twelve times.

Psychics can also be moody. One minute, we're the life of the party; the next, we just want to be left alone.

Sure you're the life of the party for the first ten minutes, but that's because the word hasn't yet gotten out that there's a psychic at the party. You get to mingle, say hello, walk around, make a comment or two, and nobody gives you the "does that have meaning?" vibe people tend to give when they find out you're a psychic.

But sooner or later, somebody will come up and start asking questions. Dumb questions, questions we've all heard a zillion times. The word gets out, the weirdness starts, and that's when we want to flee like Deadheads at a Taylor Swift concert. But that first ten minutes? Oh baby!

Because of the constant information we get, we fidget and move about. We're not always comfortable in our skin.

A lot of us are heavy or fat. The weight feels grounding, like the lead sinker that holds down a helium balloon.

Others drink, gamble, or sleep around. One of the best psychics I ever knew did all three. He eventually lost his gifts and his life, but for him, the vices were the only way to deal with the voices. Many psychics drink to silence the voices or calm their minds, but it doesn't always work.

Others have found us aloof or spacy or even unsocial, but they don't understand that there's usually more than one conversation going on when we meet people.

We call ourselves lightworkers or mediums or channels. "Love and light" means "have a nice day." The Universe means God. We don't just live our life, we go on journeys. We throw around words like *chakras*, *Reiki*, and *auras*. A porthole has nothing to do with boats and Mercury retrograde isn't the name of a band, although it should be. We get our charts done. We find twin flames. We regress.

Most psychics try to act normal and have normal conversations to fit in. But when you have three or four dead people talking to you about all the issues and woes of the person you've just met, it gets complicated. It becomes almost impossible to pay attention to a living person talking about their best friend's new hairdo when the dead people around them are talking about cancer.

So How Does This Work?
What Separates Psychics from Each Other?

In a word, filters. We all have different filters. They come from our life experiences, what we were taught, or what we want for others.

Let's start with *my* filter. I never wanted to be a psychic, not even a little. My mom and her teachers wanted this for me. They thought since the information came so easily to me, I had to do it. I saw auras at an early age and I saw spirits constantly. I knew things were going to happen before they happened and I could feel and hear people's thoughts before I could ride a two-wheeler. Once I realized everybody didn't feel these things, I saw it as a punishment. As a kid, I thought psychics were a joke. They were weird, heavy-thinking people with no sense of humor. I hated that. I felt it added unnecessary drama to an already dramatic field. It made me weird, my family weird, everything weird. I wanted to prove that all this stuff wasn't real and that it was just the imagination of lonely, gullible people.

But the more I saw, the more I realized that the people who didn't believe were the true idiots. It was far easier to prove this was real than to prove that it wasn't.

I gave in and I started doing readings. But just know that my filter is tainted with my resentment at having this so-called *gift*. In my mind, it's one of the lesser gifts handed out. Like if Santa dug around his empty bag and pulled out a used comb, that's what it feels like for me to be a psychic.

I believe in sharing psychics. There are plenty of times I can't get something on a person. Maybe I'm having a bad day, or maybe I want to go golfing and the thought of giving a reading makes me a little sick. Or maybe another psychic is supposed to do the reading because their words will be more effective.

That's not normal in my world, to refer people to someone else. Most psychics want to believe their words are divinely inspired, that they are the only ones qualified to give you the information, because it's coming from God. It goes from God, to them, to you. Nobody else, just them.

I've had people ask me to please not let anybody know they came to me, because they were worried their psychic would find out and not talk to them anymore. Fuck that. If you ever have a psychic threaten not to see you if you go to someone else, please tell them Michael Bodine thinks they're an asshole! They won't care, but it tickles my heart just thinking you might tell them.

I get why people want to covet their clients. You work really hard to make sure the reading goes well and it hurts your feelings when they think somebody else will do a better job. But it's really not about the psychic. It's always about the message.

Don't Squeeze the Shaman

I'm not a big fan of religion. I think if psychics push their religious beliefs on someone else, it gets dicey. It becomes more about those beliefs than about the reading.

I know there's a God, but to me it's a force, a power. Not a man with a white beard and staff. I believe it's a presence that every one of us can tap into if we ask. I have felt the power and felt the love, and was changed by it when I did.

I believe in Jesus, but I believe he was a kind, loving man who was crucified by assholes and died because of it, and not for my sins. I believe religion is about power and control.

I believe these things because I observe. I see the wars and crime and hatred created by religion. I feel the judgments from people who are religious, the hypocrisy. "A bible in one hand and a gun in the other" kind of thinking. And the moral belief that somehow their God is better than your God.

In my experience, religion has caused pain. My mother was confronted by so-called Christians her whole life, as is my sister, as am I. Even in my own family I have a relative who is a serious right-wing Christian, and we have to be careful not to mention what we do in front of him because it upsets him. In fact, he prefers we not mention we're even related to him when we do public speaking because he's that uncomfortable.

That's what bothers me the most about religion. The fear. How in the hell are people so afraid of the devil if their God is so all-powerful?

Religion, in all its good intention, has been just the opposite of what I assumed it was meant to be.

This isn't to say psychics don't have spiritual representatives. We do. They are called shamans, and in many ways, they act as a sort of spiritual base for the psychic community.

The first time I met a shaman I was probably around eleven years old. It was at one of those psychic camps my mother would drag me to. That particular camp was about the higher purpose of being a psychic. Spirituality, God, Rah, whatever being it was that brought you closer to pure love and understanding. Fun stuff for an eleven-year-old.

There were ministers, new age people, hippies. There were educated people, not-so-educated people, people of all different colors and backgrounds, all interested in getting closer to God.

A woman was speaking on a stage seventy-five feet in front of where my mother and I were standing, talking about her experiences finding God. She had that "God is in me" vibe. When I looked around at the crowd gathered to hear her speak, they all blended in, they all had that same vibe, as though maybe with everybody being together, the group would attract higher souls and maybe they would get answers. It felt that way to me, an atmosphere of excitement.

Except this one guy who was by himself, sitting in the corner, hitting a drum. The drumming caught my attention first because you don't see a lot of people just hitting a drum, especially when people are listening to a speaker, but nobody seemed to mind. But then I noticed he didn't seem as excited or concerned as the rest of the group. He seemed content just hitting his drum.

I tapped my mother on the shoulder, as she was concentrating on the current speaker, and asked her who this Ringo was. She gave me a "What the hell are you talking about?" face and I pointed to the guy hitting the drum. She paused for a second and then said, "Oh, he's a shaman honey, he's like a Native American holy man," and she went back to watching the person on stage.

"Really?" I said. "Does he have a band?" She looked back at me, not in the mood to answer my stupid question, and told me to go ask him myself, then went back to watching the speaker.

Normally my mother didn't trust me, unescorted, to talk to anyone in a place like that, because I had a tendency to embarrass myself or the person I talked to. But either she was so enthralled by the speaker and didn't want to be interrupted or she didn't think whatever I could say or do would upset the drum-pounding shaman. Either way, I wasn't going to let the opportunity pass to be charming, so I went over to start a conversation.

"I hear you're a shaman," I said. "How'd you get that job?" He lifted his head and gazed at me with a smile. He continued to beat his drum. He put up his finger to indicate he just needed a moment, and after ten seconds or so he stopped beating his drum, put the drumstick down, and said a quick prayer to himself. He then greeted me with another smile and told me to sit.

My first intention was to get a quick explanation and be on my way, but as with everything in that world, there was no such thing as a quick explanation. I knew if I sat I might be there a while, and normally I would have declined. But there was nothing else to do, my mom was in a trance, and I was in the middle of nowhere. "Screw it," I thought, "I'll chat with the shaman."

I sat down and folded my legs like his. He looked to be in his mid to late twenties, he had shoulder-length, light brown hair, a medium build, and an overall pleasantness to him. He extended his hand and said his name was Shamus. I shook his hand and introduced myself, but before I took my next breath I had to mention his title. "You're Shamus the shaman?" I asked with a grin. "Yeah," he said, unfazed by my ignorance. He asked why I was there.

I went into the story of my mother and how she would drag me to different psychic camps all over the country so I could be more evolved and complete. He replied with the usual "your mom sounds cool" talk and we eventually got back to my original question: what is a shaman?

He told me he didn't seek out being a shaman, but rather Spirit sought him out. He said he started having dreams that Spirit wanted his service, then started hearing voices and seeing signs. All of this sounded like the typical story I heard from people back then: Spirit coming to them, asking them to trust their inner voice, their eyes. But this guy said he was told to go to the woods and find a hollow tree. He was told to put his clenched hand inside the tree and keep it there overnight. He said if Spirit wanted him to become a shaman, Spirit would leave something in his hand the next day. So, he did what he was told. And the next day when he took his hand out of the hollow tree, he opened his fist and there was a clump of moss with a single bud.

He said he decided to study with medicine men and participate in different Native American ceremonies. He said he had a long way to go before his path was truly shown to him, but he felt at peace knowing he was at least on a path.

I asked him about the drumming and he said it was a form of meditation, prayer. He said he felt it called ancient spirits and elders, and it helped calm him.

I liked him. I really didn't care much for most of the people I met there, but I did like this guy. I liked him because he didn't try to sell me anything, he didn't patronize me, he wasn't mental, and because he felt real, like he was just as amazed at all of this as I was. I could feel his strength.

Since that time, I've met many other shamans, some more believable than others. Some seemed to have an agenda, some just called themselves shamans to fit in.

I was once at event with a bunch of different healers, psychics, and spiritualists a while back and I ran into a guy on my way out to the car to get more things. He was leaning against the wall with an unlit cigarette in his mouth, digging for a light. He asked me if I had a match. I don't smoke, but I happened to have a lighter for candles, so I gave it to him.

He was about forty years old, thin, with long, scraggly hair and dark eyes. He was wearing a suit, but it looked like he'd been wearing it for a month straight. He looked beat up, tired. He lit his cigarette and learned back against the wall. He said thank you, and as I was walking away, he stopped me. "Hey," he said, "aren't you Michael Bodine?" I stopped and said I was. A smile came across his face. "I've heard of you," he said.

"I hope it was good," I shot back and he motioned me over to chat. "Oh yeah, all good," and he extended his hand. "I'm Carl," he said, "Carl the shaman."

I laughed to myself. "You're a shaman?" I asked.

He said, "Oh yeah, got the calling years ago." He took a deep drag from his cigarette and exhaled as if to release all the years of torment he had gone through. "It's been hard," he said softly.

"Damn, Carl," I replied, "I'm sorry," and I tried to give him the best "I care" vibe I could muster. "Well," he said as he looked down, coughed up something from the bottom of his liver, and spat it out, "it's a calling."

I had the sense that he wanted to carry on the conversation, talk war stories, but I almost threw up from watching him spit and I was truly in a hurry. I wanted to get out of there as quick as I could. "Callings can suck, Carl," I said as I motioned to move, "but it was nice to meet you."

He saw I wanted to go and I could see the disappointment in his face. Again, he took a deep drag from his cigarette. "No worries," he said. "I gotta pick up my old lady at the strip club anyway."

Now I'm feeling sorry for the guy. I put my arms out to give him a hug, but he recoiled. "Sorry man," he said, "I'm not a big hugger."

"Of course not," I thought to myself, and that was the last I saw of Carl the shaman.

If you come across a person who says they're a shaman, use your intuition. Just like with everybody else in this field, you have your Shamuses and you have your Carls.

I don't care if you're an atheist or a Christian, if you pray to Allah or a pumpkin, I respect whatever your beliefs are.

I also don't believe it's a choice to be gay, though some psychics do. I think it's a gene thing. In the simplest terms, I believe there are two sides—one very gay side and one not gay at all side, and all sorts of degrees in between. If you have a little gay in you, maybe you do have a choice, but in my mind, it's not really a choice. And honestly, I don't care. I feel bad for some gay people because I know they struggle with it.

One of my favorite people in the world, someone I greatly admire, struggled for years because he was married, had three kids, and was bisexual. You couldn't find a more understanding, intelligent, and responsible man. But when it all came out that he was bi and his wife told his world, all his fears were justified. After three years, two of his adult kids still won't talk to him.

But I don't always live as my higher self. I've let negative influences affect my judgment before, too.

I walked into a McDonald's one day. I was in a hurry, hungry, and not in the mood. The only thing I wanted was a Big Mac, hold the onions. The last time I was there, I ordered the same thing, but instead of holding the onions, they piled them on. This time I was ready, I was going to make sure they held the onions, even if I had to watch them actually hold them. The person who was helping me was not a native English speaker. I was short on time and was already frustrated with the time spent waiting in line. I tried several times to explain what I wanted, but every time I repeated it, he only shook his head and looked lost.

My patience was nonexistent and asked another person to come and help, because obviously this guy was struggling, but they were too busy with someone else, so I was stuck with this guy.

I could see his anger at me, which in turn further pissed me off.

Finally, I told him to forget it. I was pissed, he was pissed, and we both gave each other the stink eye as I walked out.

I couldn't help thinking what an asshole this guy was for being mad at me. Clearly I was the victim here. Wasn't the customer always supposed to be right?

When I got to my car I was still bugged. Something wasn't right, I knew that. But I kept trying to pinpoint what it was. I went over it and over it, and finally I asked my guides what was the dang deal.

I always forget not to ask these questions unless I really want the answer. When you talk to spirit guides all day they aren't shy about sharing their perspective, and in this case it was like they put me right inside his soul. Suddenly I felt his unhappiness, his anguish. I could feel his fear and embarrassment at not being able to speak our language. I felt his loneliness at being so far from his home. I could feel how badly he missed his life, but I could also feel how hard his life back home really was. I knew he was going to give up, quit. And I could hear his worry at what he was going to tell his sister when he quit. The anger and hopelessness was overwhelming, and to top it all off, I could see how he saw me.

A privileged, spoiled white man, with no patience or understanding of other people. The guides were kind enough to also point out that he was learning another language, while I could barely speak English. All this as I was driving down the freeway. I went from feeling self-righteous in my anger to being ashamed at my own ignorance.

If that wasn't enough, they also pointed out the missed opportunity. I could have been kind, I could have smiled and eased his mind. I could have somehow reminded him how impressive it was that he was learning another language when I only knew one. I could have told him to hang in there, that he would get it, but instead I gave him the stink eye and probably the final excuse to give up. That haunted me for a long time, not only how I was, but the missed opportunity to make someone else feel better. It still bothers me, and I won't do that again.

So, my filters are just like everyone else's—influenced by my experiences. The stuff I don't know could fill the barney blue. But I'm open to learning.

Some psychics are very religious, so when they do a reading, they tend to refer to God a lot, or suggest that you may need more God in your life, if they think you don't have enough.

Some psychics are into fitness or taking care of your body, so they may make a comment or two about your looks or physical appearance, maybe even suggest you get into better shape. Other psychics may not be comfortable with gay people or the Amish or another group of people, so that thinking gets in the way of a proper reading.

If you go to a psychic who doesn't share your mindset, try another one. You'll find one who understands your lifestyle.

These issues have nothing to do with Spirit. Spirit is way beyond the ignorance we humans have. They couldn't care less if you sing show tunes, or if you believe the world is only two thousand years old. They don't judge you, they love you with all their being. Their only hope is that you feel better about your experience here, while you are still here.

It's not our job to judge people. There are psychics out there that make people cry because they didn't like their appearance or sexual orientation.

I know this because they come to me, nervous, thinking I will do the same thing.

Maybe the next time you get a reading and the psychic tells you to mix in a salad or repent your sins, you'll know it's not coming from Spirit but rather someone who needs to clean their filter.

The Different Types of Psychics and What They Do

Some people don't know that there are many different types of psychics and we don't all do the same thing.

For instance, many people assume I can help locate their pets, wallets, rings and other stuff because I'm a psychic; psychics are just supposed to know that stuff.

I would love to help people find whatever they lost, but first I have to find *my* wallet, *my* ring, and *my* house. I lose things all the time. This doesn't make me a bad psychic; it makes it frustrating to hang out with me or be in a hurry to get somewhere when I can't find my keys.

And yes, I know psychics who do find things, but maybe they suck at seeing the future.

My point is that we all do things a little differently and we all pick up things in different ways.

You have your mediums (who talk to the dead), your channelers (who *become* the dead), and your intuitives (who sense what's happening). You have seers (who use objects to see your life). You have the past life people, the present-day people, and your future folks.

Some psychics find bodies (I hate that job) and some talk to cats. You have healers who are psychic, and you have the general all-purpose psychics who do a little of it all. That's the category I fall more into.

No two psychics are the same, just like no two people are really the same. They each offer different services and each one is different from the other.

The darlings of the group are the mediums. People love a good medium. They talk to your friends and relatives on the other side, and they confirm, through the information they give you, that there is life after death. And they have a spooky, eerie vibe to them that gives you the impression something cool is about to happen.

They're called mediums for just that reason: they're a link between the living and the dead. That's also how a lot of them get their information: the deceased actually show up and start talking to them. Regular all-purpose psychics have that once in a while, but mediums experience that most of the time.

The media loves mediums. They're dramatic, they got spunk, and there's a feeling of showmanship when you watch them perform, like you're watching a magic show, except it's actually real most of the time.

And they can really be impactful. When you've got a good medium working the room, pulling stuff seemingly out of nowhere, telling you about how your mother died or a childhood memory or a name that fits, it can blow your mind. You scratch your head trying to figure out how they knew the stuff they did.

Now the skeptical types will assume it all came from the internet. That when you bought your ticket the medium looked you up on Google and got the info they needed, and then threw out your info hoping you'd get it. And I'm sure that does happen.

But it doesn't happen all the time. I've been to mediums that wouldn't have a clue what the internet was, I've been to mediums before there was an internet, and they still knew things. There is some amazing talent out there and they are very real.

When I was a kid, true mediums were rare. They were much more underground than they are today and they did their work in small, private groups. You had to be very quiet when you went to a medium, so they could concentrate on the messages. They didn't ask questions. They made statements such as "There's a person here whose name is Frank, and he died of a heart attack and he wants his daughter to know he's okay. His daughter is in this part of the room," and they'd point to a part of the room. Then they'd go on to someone else. Their job was to reassure people that their loved ones were still around them, that they still cared, and that they would visit them from time to time. This could be tremendously helpful to people because they would find peace of mind.

It's a great beginning to understanding Spirit and what's out there. But that's what a medium is to me: the beginning. Some mediums claim they can also give predictions and some psychics also claim to be mediums. It can get confusing. I think what happens is that some mediums are told by the dead around them what's going to happen to someone and some psychics talk to your relatives who just show up. But in my little head, mediums talk to your friends and relatives who have passed and a psychic gives predictions and fills in the blanks. I say talking to Uncle Harry about his gout is boring as hell, but if that's what floats your boat, more power to you.

The problem for me is that too many of the so-called "real mediums" ask so many questions. They fish. They don't directly address the person they're giving the information to. For instance, they ask the group if anyone knows a Frank, or they ask the group if anybody lost a father to a heart attack, instead of telling them.

Mediums also tend to have more of a God complex. I get it, it's hard not to be a diva when somebody is always blowing smoke up your ass, but it goes against the whole evolved thing we're supposed to be practicing.

The famous ones won't give you the time of day. I know my sister has dealt with the some of the biggies and they've turned out to be assholes, or at least they were to her. Now she would never admit that; she sees good in everyone. But based on how they treated her and how they acted with her, it was pretty clear to me that these folks needed a time out.

They hold huge events and charge a lot of dough, but only connect with a few people in the audience. I'm sure in their mind it's justified entertainment. But I think it loses that intimacy and authenticity. And a part me even understands why these divas turn into assholes. I'm sure they have a ton of people bugging them all the time for the stupidest things and they just want to be left alone. I even get bugged and I'm underground.

But get a friggin' handler or at least don't be such a blatant dick to people.

This profession isn't strong enough yet to handle arrogance like that. It doesn't do anybody any good to have you walking around thinking you're better than everybody else.

It also leaves the door wide open for the ignorant skeptics to come in and judge *all* psychics by their actions. I'm not saying psychics aren't also divas; there are more and more of them popping up all the time. But I prefer the humble ones. They seem to get it more than the divas.

Channelers are the performance artists of the group. The very first channelers I saw when I was a kid were amazing. Like mediums, their job was to show you that Spirit existed. They did this by allowing a spirit to come inside them, like a positive possession. The fun thing was watching them transform from who they were when they came in to whatever spirits would enter their bodies! These people would actually change right in front of you. Even their hair color would change. You were so busy being amazed that you barely listened to what they had to say, which was usually, "Love is good, we are God, and don't forget to tip your waiter on the way out." It was some generic message, but who cares? It was a great show. If you didn't believe in Spirit after that, you were just ridiculous.

But now, channelers are people who claim to have Spirit speak through them. They don't really change, but just kind of perform the reading instead. Now the benefit of this is that it's way more dramatic than your average reading. You get a show *and* a reading. Other channelers don't actually perform the reading, but "channel" certain people—usually famous ones like Albert Einstein or Cleopatra. Sometimes the title of the person they're channeling might be "Orf the warrior" or "Barf the apprentice." But you'll never get "Bob from accounting." The names have to be interesting, mystical. Whatever the name they choose, bring some popcorn and enjoy the performance. If you can get past the gyrations (which I never could), listen to the message. It's a good time.

The next group is seers. This group isn't as flashy as your mediums or channelers, but they're visual. They use tarot cards, tea leaves, chicken bones, and yes, the occasional crystal ball. These were my favorite psychics when I was a kid because they tended to be more traditional, less flashy. It's hard to be stuck up with chicken bones in your pocket. And they seemed interested in whatever they got.

My mother was a tarot reader. First, she would ask you to shuffle her deck until you were told to stop. Now most times a voice never told you to stop, you just got sick of shuffling. But in her mind that was the same thing. She would then hold the deck in her hands and give you a reading first before looking at the cards, and then she would begin. She used the cards as more of a guide; not for her, but for the person getting the reading. Each card had pictures on it, some with more details than others. She would point out things in your life that correlated to the cards. If you were feeling blue, she would point out the person on the card who had their head down and explain that it was you. For some people, the cards really helped. She didn't need them, but they suited her personality.

Tea leafers and chicken boners, rune users and crystal ballers all work along the same lines that tarot card people do, but they see things that a non-psychic person doesn't always see. I like a good bone seer, because they don't care whether you like what they have to say or not. They do their thing: they hand you old, creepy bones and ask you to hold them. Then they tell you to toss them on the table, and then they study them. They see pictures and images just based on how they land or where they end up.

I'd just see bones when I look at them, but a good seer can see everything from your first love to your biggest fear. It's surprising how accurate those people can be.

Same thing with tea leaf people. They give you a cup of tea, you drink it, and when you're done the tea leaves are at the bottom. They can tell you what's going on with your life by seeing pictures in the leaves.

I always liked the idea of it: drinking tea, relaxing, and getting a reading. Again, it wasn't about the leaves; it was about what the psychic was getting. But the personal touch made it interesting, at least to me. They just used whatever medium they had to express it.

Now we get to the average Joe psychics, the water boys of the group. This is where I fall.

Unlike the first few groups, these people don't have a lot of flair. They may wear mirrors around their necks and like breathable clothes, but flair? Not so much. Mediums are lousy with flair, maybe too much for some. Channelers have flair, but mostly in their performance; they tend to be broad in their strokes. And seers? Well, they just look around a lot, like Japanese tourists at a Hooters.

The water boy psychics can be a bit boring compared to the others. You can walk by one and not even know they're a psychic. Mediums will come right up and scare the crap out of you. Regular psychics are more reserved most of the time; they use sunscreen and most of them tend to be hippyish, earthy people. They know their place is on the sidelines, giving you hope and encouragement. Newer ones are more enthusiastic, but generally speaking, your average Joe or Jane psychic is pretty reserved. Most people who come to us are thirsty—some very thirsty—for knowledge. Our job is to quench that thirst with hope and prove that there's love and power around them. Tell them that they are on the right path or the wrong one and how to fix it. We're cheerleaders, we spur you on with data about your lives, past and present. We point out the future opportunities to give you that hope, so when you walk away you feel better inside, calmer, reassured.

We aren't better or worse than the other psychics, we just offer a different package.

I don't mean to leave out the pet psychics, I just don't know that much about them. My sister Nikki used to talk to animals. When she first told me, I thought she was off her rocker, but the people who came to her were really helped, they swore by her. She could tell what was bothering the person's pet and how to treat them; she just knew. It wasn't my cup of tea—I have a hard enough time with people. But who can argue with results?

How Can You Tell the Good Ones from the Bad?

Part of the learning process when it came to being a psychic and getting answers was actually getting readings. It was important to get the perspective of the person being read before you were the reader. At least that's what I was told.

Everybody does readings in different ways. Some are floaty, some are direct, some you don't know what they hell they are. But if you observed someone getting a reading, you could see what worked and what didn't.

When I would come home from school, my mother would whisk me into the kitchen, where all the budding new psychics were hanging out, practicing their talents and discovering their chakras. New "clients" were hard to come by back then because psychics were considered evil. Packs of Christians and Jehovah's Witnesses would patrol the neighborhoods, looking for stray cats and converts. You didn't dare advertise or draw attention to yourself as a psychic! Salem of 1692 was just like yesterday to some of these people; you had to be careful not to light a match around some of them. Everything had to stay on the hush-hush. When someone we didn't recognize came over, they always had to have a reference. We didn't want any riffraff. That left slim pickings for people to practice on. They only had each other; when a fresh body walked into the room, it was like a pack of wolves looking at a steak.

For me, it was nice to be wanted, but I learned quickly that it wasn't about me—they just needed somebody, anybody with a pulse.

My mother would purposely steer me to the one who was most accurate that day. She knew my attention span was akin to a squirrel at a hoedown, so her best bet was putting me with someone who could keep my attention.

When I first started being the guinea pig, it was kind of fun. They were learning, I was learning, and when they got something right it was exciting for both of us. Like when you put a puzzle together: "That goes there; this goes here; oh fun, I can see it now." That sort of thing.

I found myself rooting for people to get things correct. Even if the person was off, I tried to make it work. If they said I was good in math even though I was flunking, I would say, "Well, I was good in math *class* today, I didn't get kicked out. So yeah, I was good in math." Anything to encourage them. I wanted to be a good little guinea pig. I wanted them to feel good about what they were picking up.

But apparently my approach was the wrong way to go. Our teacher, Birdie, thought false encouragement was more harmful than good. I think her exact words were, "Michael, do you want people to lie to you? Then don't lie to them." Birdie, or Buzzkill, as I liked to call her, hated inexactitude. She wanted people to be clear on what they got, to the point, not fluffy.

So, after our chat I started being more critical. I started asking for more information, not just generalities. It was from those experiences that I learned how to be the kind of psychic I would want to go see. Blunt, to the point. I didn't like all the bullshit theatrics; I didn't see it as necessary. If you had the information, I needed to hear it.

One of my favorite psychics back then was just like that. He didn't care if people liked him or not; he said whatever came into his head. He wasn't for everybody. In fact, I think he pissed off more people than he helped, but maybe that's another reason I liked him.

The first time we talked I sat down and said hi. He looked me over and said, "So, what are you, ten?"

"Yeah, about that," I replied.

"Well, what the hell do you want to know? If the Easter bunny is real? Well I got bad news for you, kid."

"No," I said, "I don't want to know anything. I want to go watch *Gilligan's Island*, but my mother's making me do this."

"Who's your mom?" he asked.

"Mae, the one that lives here," I sarcastically replied.

His demeanor changed and a smile came across his face. "Oh, you must be Mikey."

"Yeah." I said back. "So whatever you got to say, go ahead and say it so I can get out of here."

He laughed. "Look kid, you're ten, you're going to go through so many changes in the next few years it would take a month to explain, so do us both a favor and go watch Gilligan." Then he gave me that "sorry, but come on" look and went back to reading his *Seth Speaks* book.

I was surprised but impressed; everybody else tried to woo me in the hopes that I would report back how great they were. This guy couldn't have cared less.

I thought to myself that if I ever did this stuff, *that's* how I wanted to be.

As I got older I grew to like him even more, but he struggled with alcohol and drugs, and one day he just stopped coming by. I don't know exactly what happened to him, but the rumor was that he drank himself to death. I think he was just one of those people who couldn't deal with all the voices he heard.

Budding psychics aren't always exact. If fact, they tend to be extremely vague because they don't trust themselves with the information. They feel things out, they second-guess.

They want to sound confident, so some of them speak with more authority, but that doesn't make them more accurate.

There was a guy I used to call "Oh boy Bob." The first time I sat down to talk to him, he looked at me, then looked down, and then said, "Oh boy, this is bad." I sat there and stared at him; nobody had ever done that before. "What do you mean, bad?" I asked.

"Well," he said, "it just feels bad when I look at your face." I stood up and yelled for my mom. One of the perks of having a reading at your house when you're ten is that you can yell for your mother when things freak you out. My mom came over and asked me what was wrong. I told her, Bob here thinks something bad is going to happen to me. My mother smiled and calmly asked Bob what he was picking up. Bob seemed tortured. He kept shaking his head, closing his eyes like he was trying to remember and forget something all at the same time.

"See mom?" I said. "I think I'm going to die!"

"No honey, you're not going to die." She then asked Bob again what he was picking up. He paused for a month and then finally said, "I think you're going to get a surprise test in math tomorrow."

I looked at Bob, I looked at my mom, then back at Bob. "Okay, that's it!" I exclaimed. "I'm going over to Bobby's house." And I got up and left.

I practically soiled myself thinking all sorts of terrible things and this guy was spazzing over a math test. That's the thing about readings; it can be a nerve-racking experience. I knew most of what these people were picking up was hit or miss, but even a broken clock is right twice a day. What if Bob was on to something?

Every time I got a reading from Bob he did the same thing. He'd start off by saying, "Oh boy, this doesn't look good," or "Oh boy, this is bad," but it always turned out to be something simple. I forgot to feed the dog or my bike was going to get a flat.

I think for Bob it was about getting your attention, not necessarily about what he had to say. I still know psychics like that today.

Bob eventually went into the insurance game, and as far as I know, he did okay. I think his "holy crap this is bad" approach worked better for him in that line of work. Still, I am grateful to him. Since getting readings from Bob, I take them all with a grain of salt.

Even with the different kinds of psychics, there are also different kinds of personalities and experiences.

There are the people who are just starting out. I call them "newbies." To me, these are the people who have only been doing it for a little while. They have that fresh, new, psychic glow. Their eyes are bright and they have a firm command of the English language. They have a spring in their step, an excitement to their words, and a genuine enthusiasm for what they do. They can't wait to answer your questions because it's all so fascinating. They know everything there is to know within hours of becoming psychic, and a few of them you want to punch in the face.

Some newbies only last a couple of years or so. Some come out of the gate after just a few classes thinking they are now professional psychics.

A lot of those people burn out quickly, having realized how hard this job really is. If they get through the first five years, they usually stay.

Then there are the people who have been doing it fifteen to twenty years. They've got a nice rhythm, they know what they can do and what they can't do. They're more tempered than your average newbie, not as excited; but still, they have an interest in what they do. They care.

Maybe some of them feel like they're in a rut, like "Jesus, this was just supposed to be a hobby and here I am twenty years later," but they don't come off like that. The ego suit has pretty much worn off by then. Some can come off as entitled, but they have their niche and it works. So, in my opinion, your middle psychic has a nice blend—not too eager, not too jaded.

Then there are the ones who have been doing it awhile.

Imagine you're a chef and you make a really good burger. I'm not talking about your ordinary, run-of-the-mill burger, but a melt in your mouth, "holy crap, this is good" burger. And it's exciting that you can make this burger. Yes, there are a ton of burgers out there, but yours is really good. And you love the compliments you get from people who are just trying your burger. It's unique, it's fun, it satisfies that hunger like nothing they've tried, and everybody wants one. They write stories about your burger. It's on TV and talk shows. You are truly a great chef for having the ability to make such a great burger.

Okay, now imagine that a couple years go by. People are still loving your burger and they still can't believe how great it is, but when you hear that, it doesn't have the same weight. They still do stories about your burger, but they only want to talk about how it all began and you've told that story so many times you're starting to get tired of it. Still, it is a pretty good burger and it has been good to you, so you keep smiling and making the burger.

Now imagine forty years go by. You're still making that same damn burger. You tried making omelets and pancakes. You even tried making spaghetti. But nobody wanted any of those; they just want that same, stinking burger you've made a million times. It's a curse now, not a blessing. When people tell you how wonderful it is, you don't feel joy and excitement. You just want to smash it in their face and twist it while the cheese drips slowly off their chin. But you can't, because you're known for that burger. It's tied to your name. What else would you do after forty years?

So you keep making them, and while half of you is praying people will still like them, the other half is hoping you have a stroke.

Toasty psychics walk around with their eyes half shut and their lower lips slight drooping. They get bored and impatient easily. When they do get information, they say it quickly, so they don't forget it. Their only goal in starting a reading is to get it over with as fast as they can so they can go watch a movie and eat bad food. They don't care if the information changes your life; they've heard that shit a million times.

But they're good, man are they good. They've got the signs down pat, they've got the bullshit figured out, and they know what you're going to say before you say it.

So each kind has good and bad points. The newbies are excited and fresh, but not very experienced. They may not know all the nuances yet, but they make up for it with passion.

The middle folks are steady: they know their shit and they care, but maybe they get a bit predictable. Nothing wrong with that.

And your burnt-out psychics are grumpy; they just want to tell you the info and get out. They *are* accurate, they *are* to the point, and they think you're stupid if you don't listen.

There are some other things you should know when you decide who to go to.

First, there's the question of where the best psychics are located. Some say California psychics are better than New York psychics or midwestern psychics are more real than southern psychics. What's true is that California psychics are more laid back because they live in frickin' California! Eastern psychics are more blunt because that's how people are in the East. Midwest psychics are more grounded because midwestern people tend to be that way, and southern psychics are more traditional because that's how they are down South. It doesn't mean one group is more evolved or better than the next. It means those are the filters you'll receive your reading through. You want a more grounded reading, call someone from the Midwest. You want a little gumbo with your cards, call the South.

Whenever I go to California, I get booked a lot, because people want a different point of view than the ones they get from the Cali psychics. Not better, just different.

There's also a rotten side of the community.

Some psychics like to bad-mouth other psychics; it's actually pretty common. With more and more psychics out there and more of a battle for your third eye dough, it's tough. People look for an edge, and a lot of them don't mind throwing another psychic under the bus to find it.

Another psychic wrote a book two years after my first book came out and used the same title. He knew about my book, he just didn't care.

To a lot of psychics, it's about business, and that's all.

I've heard terrible things about myself throughout the years—horrible things about my character, my readings, my sexual orientation. I get that it's better to be talked about than not to be talked about at all, but some of it's not even true!

Then there are the competitive psychics. They enter competitions to see who's the best. You'll see them all over. "The best psychic in so-and-so." I never understood that, because anybody who has done this for more than five years knows there are so many things that determine what a good reading is. It's like "so-and-so is the best lover." Nobody is the best lover for everybody; it's about the connection, the chemistry, the trust. All those things determine what a good reading is and everybody is different.

It's not about the psychic. We are just the messengers. Those competitions are about who the psychics know and how many people they have following them, not about their abilities. But because psychics are looking for an edge, they do that stuff.

Others call themselves masters. That's another stupid thing, because one of the first laws of spirituality is humility. If you go around calling yourself a master, it means you missed lesson number one.

I am acutely aware of all the fake, phony, lying, conning shysters out there in the psychic community. I'm reminded of them every time I'm introduced as a psychic. A lot of people assume it's all fake and a way to con the weak and vulnerable. It's easier to think that than to take it seriously, because that kind of thinking opens up a big can of worms, and I get that. But anything that makes us look fake or phony makes it harder for the ones who are legit. And there are a lot of legit, good psychics out there (and they don't all smell like patchouli).

Do your research, get referrals, and remember just to take what makes sense to you. It has to feel right. If it's just advice, tell them you already have a Magic 8-Ball. If they ask too many questions, suggest *they* pay *you*. Don't be afraid of coincidence. If you're thinking about getting a reading and your friend calls you up out of the blue and says she just saw a psychic who blew her mind, put two and two together. That's how these things work sometimes.

What's the Best Way to Get the Most out of Your Reading?

When you do decide to get a reading, go in with an open mind. It doesn't have to be completely open; a little skepticism is a good thing when you get a reading. But don't walk in with a "fuck you" attitude. Psychics can feel that.

Newbies get nervous, middle ones get impatient, and toasty psychics get pissed. Leave a little wiggle room.

If you want specific answers, ask specific questions. So many people come to me and say, "Just tell me what you get." That's like going to a restaurant and telling the waiter, "Bring me what you feel like."

What I tell people who say that to me is, "At least give me an area to start with." Love, health, work, travel, something, anything. I don't need information, I need a direction.

In fact, for me, too much information screws up my head. I start thinking about things and then it all gets goofy.

Have questions.

Don't start off talking about how wonderful the last psychic you went to was. If they were so wonderful, why didn't you go back?

I know a lot of people go to more than one psychic. I have no problem with that, but don't set up a competition. Again, it's about the message, not the messenger.

I'm a future guy, I deal mostly with events to come. The most maddening thing to me is when a person is presented with an opportunity, but they refuse to see it.

For me, the best readings are when the person gets it, when they see the opportunities and are willing to take advantage of them.

The ones that suck are the people who try to trick you. They tell you false information in hopes they can trip you up. I've done many readings where the person will ask me about their kids when they don't have any or ask about their relationship when they're not in one. I've had celebrities disguise their voices to try to confuse me or say they're straight when they're gay.

Psychics are supposed to give you hope, hope that there's meaning to your life, hope that things will work out, hope that you're not alone in your day-to-day life. They're also there to help you with answers, things that you can't just figure out alone.

You can do what you want when you get a reading, but if you're looking for answers, just like everything else, you get what you put in.

I walked into a fast-food restaurant not long ago to grab a snack. It was noon and the place was packed with people coming and going, getting their food, everything efficient and not a lot of warmth. But the girl helping us did have warmth. She was friendly, bright, easy to talk to, and one of those people who actually cared whether you were there or not.

Most people didn't have time for her pleasantries—they just wanted their food so they could get on with their day—but her personality didn't go unnoticed to the man in front of me. He was a businessman wearing a suit, in his late forties or early fifties. He seemed excited to talk to her because her engaging manner was hard to ignore. They conversed a bit and as they did, he asked her if she'd ever been in sales. She smiled and said no, that this was in fact her first job. She said she'd thought about sales, but the opportunity never came up. He pulled out his card and presented it to her. He owned a small but thriving company and told her he thought with her personality and charm, she would be a perfect fit for a position he was looking to fill. She smiled and thanked the man. She got his food and, as he took it, he suggested she look his company up online and contact him if she was interested.

She again thanked the man and waved to him as he took his food and left. She greeted me with a smile and proceeded to ask me what I would like. I told her what I wanted and she chatted with me while she added it all up. As she waited for my food to come, her coworker came up to her and started to complain that she just didn't think she wanted to keep working there. The long hours and hard work were taking their toll, and she asked the girl what she thought. The girl paused for a bit and said, "Oh I can't keep doing this either, but I have no clue what else I could do."

The card was literally still warm in her pocket from the owner of a company who would hire her on the spot and she didn't know what else she could do?!

Be willing to open your eyes.

2

ANSWERS: DOES ANYONE HAVE A CLUE?

Answers. Isn't that what this is all about? People want answers.

People always ask me how I work, how I get the information. It's a little hard to explain because so many things happen at once, but I'll try to describe it.

The first thing that happens is I think about the person's name. I either get a feel for it or I don't. If I don't, I concentrate a little harder. If nothing comes to mind and I don't get any kind of feeling, I let it go. Based on past experiences, I see that as a sign that I'm not supposed to do a reading for them.

This doesn't mean something bad is about to happen or the person is blocking me. It means for whatever reason that person doesn't need a reading from me.

If I do get a feeling about somebody, it's like an excited feeling, like I hooked up to the internet and I can feel more stuff is coming.

Then I start to get pictures and images, examples of what that person is like. For instance, I might get a picture of someone sad or excited. Someone about to have a good experience or someone who has got the world on their shoulders. These images come quick and it's about getting a general picture of the person.

What I find interesting in doing readings is that as I'm getting information and I'm describing what I'm getting, words just start coming into my head.

Some of those words I'm aware of because I'm using them to describe what I'm getting, but other words don't always make sense to me. And the more I trust myself, the more I allow the words to flow.

Another thing that happens to me is that I become that person. Not literally, but I start to see experiences they've gone through and I can also see the outcome of what they're about to do. It's like watching a movie and being in the movie at the same time. Again, all of this comes really quickly. Most times I write down the main points of what I'm seeing, so I can go back and explain it to them in a way that will make sense

Sometimes it's not just for the deep stuff. Sometimes people want to know what's wrong with their lawn mower or what they should get their wife for their anniversary. Maybe they lost their cat, or are tired all the time, or depressed.

For me, when it's simple things, I'll just get the simple answer. I'll get a picture, like where their cat is or what their wife wants. If people want deeper things I'll go there, but you can get answers anywhere. Church, friends, a lot of people go to therapy, some just travel.

And now, more and more people are going to psychics for answers. You know why?

Because where else can you ask somebody what's wrong with your lawn mower, find out where your cat is, and figure out why you're so depressed, all in one sitting? Nowhere.

You can ask a therapist why you're so depressed, but try asking them where your keys are, or ask your mechanic why you can't sleep.

Psychics answer questions; that's what we do.

And it's been that way since I was a kid. If you were looking for answers, the house I grew up in was the place to go.

Psychics of all shapes and sizes were there to answer any and all questions you might have. Little questions, big questions, it didn't matter. Was your cat depressed? They'd find out. Was your girlfriend pregnant? They'd know. Were the hometown boys going to win the big game? They'd find that out too. From "What's the key to the universe?" to

"What's this thing on my lip?" they would answer any and all questions. And if one person didn't know the answer, the person next to them did. If that person drew blanks, they consulted the stars. Anything they thought might help bring them answers, they would use.

I came in one time to see a guy wearing a pyramid on his head, singing "The Battle Hymn of the Republic." When I asked my mother what the guy was doing, she looked at me incredulously and said, "Answering a question, honey, what do you think?"

Of course he was, because that's what we do. We answer questions. Doesn't matter what it is. We'll take a stab at it.

We're like the psychological and spiritual Walmart. And we don't care what you wear when you come see us either.

We're not doctors, psychiatrists, or therapists. We can just answer more stuff than they do. We aren't confined to one way of thinking, like your average educated professional. We're psychics! It's the one good thing about not being taken seriously: we can say whatever we want.

But for those of you who take your psychic with a dash of seriousness, we can offer hope that life has meaning, hope that answers will come, hope that we're not all alone in this world.

Here's the rub: Answers will come to you whether you see a psychic or not. It's just the way it works. Psychics can help you see the possibility that the answers are coming, but we don't order them for you.

Sometimes people confuse me with Santa Claus or Google. They think since I can see, talk to, and smell Spirit, I have an "in" with them. I don't. In fact, most guides just tolerate me. If they had retinas, most of them would probably dislocate them from rolling their eyes when they meet me. They are much closer to the people they work with and listen far more intently to them than they do a smart-ass psychic like myself.

I've gotten a lot of readings over the years, from a bunch of different psychics. Some were amazing in their accuracies and encouraging manner. And some were your basic fortune cookie psychics. But no matter how good they were, or how bad, it always boiled down to me, my choices, and my actions. I still had to participate. You can't just sit back, look at your door, and hope the answers show up. You *have* to have some movement, some intent.

If you're working on a puzzle and you're struggling, you try everything, but sometimes you still just can't see it. You try looking at it different ways, maybe you even try forcing a piece in, but that turns out worse, so now you're really frustrated. You ask someone to help, a puzzle person. And sure enough, they see what you can't. It's right there, you just didn't see it. You feel relieved. You think you got it figured out. It feels easy, especially the way they did it. You feel better because you feel like you're on track.

You go back and start doing the puzzle again, but crap, you get stuck again. No worries, you can just call up your buddy and have them show you what they did last time. You call up that person who helped you before and ask them to help again. They come over and again they see the problem; they move this piece here, move that piece there, and pow, you're back on track. They leave.

You start to do the puzzle again, but you're not as committed. Even though it's your puzzle, it doesn't feel like it's all really yours anymore, because you've gotten so much help with it.

Now it becomes more about just getting it done, rather than doing it yourself. So, at the first sign of trouble you figure, screw it, I'll have my friend do it.

That's what happens with psychics: The more correct information you give someone, the more some of those people want you to make all the decisions for them. They figure if we know the answers, why don't we just tell them and save them the trouble of figuring it out? Well, for the exception of some actors, most politicians, HR supervisors, and this girl I dated in high school, people are not robots. It's not about being told what to do and doing it.

When you do that, it is no longer about their life. It's about getting through life as easy and with as much help as they can.

A side note to the divas out there: This is why all psychics—no matter how wonderful they are, no matter if they've been voted "best psychic of blah blah"—are going to suck once in a while. Doesn't mean you're a bad psychic or your gifts have been taken away. We are not here to make people dependent on us and if we don't recognize when someone is, "they"—Spirit—help us with it.

We pick up wrong information and we don't get clarity: things that give the reader pause. It's important because it gives the power back to the person and hopefully they start to trust themselves more.

Here's an analogy to make this all more clear.

You're running late and you have four minutes to get to a destination twenty minutes away. People are waiting. You're making okay time, but suddenly, at the longest stop light in North America, an SUV, just slightly smaller than an actual school bus, turns into your lane in front of you as the light finally turns green. You proceed forward, hoping that at the very least this person is in the same hurry as you are, but judging by how quickly you catch up to this airport on wheels, you're not even sure if the person is alive.

You look at the time. It's official: You're late and your sense of urgency has just been bumped up a notch. You can't go another way because the place you're going is on the same road and you can't go around because this behemoth is so big there's no room for error. You tap your feet, you slap your hands on the steering wheel, you stare at the ceiling hoping that whatever might be up there sees your frustration and takes pity on you, but apparently it goes unnoticed because now the monster truck is braking.

Surely nobody can be in front of this person. They're going too slow. You know the speed limit hasn't gone down, because you just saw the sign, and you didn't see any construction zone signs, so why on earth would they slow down?

Obviously, they must be on their phone; or worse, they're texting. Man, you *hate* people who text and drive. Of course, you text your friend about this, you've got places to be. You make the decision to go around, knowing you're going to have to take a risk and floor it. You're late, you're pissed, and it's time.

Just when your foot goes to accelerate, something very loud in your head says "NO!" It's so loud, in fact, that it makes you pause. And as you pause, you notice, to your right, a state trooper sitting on the side of the road with his speed gun pointed at all oncoming traffic. As you check your speed, a slight shockwave runs through your body and you think to yourself, *phew.*

You take back all the things you said about the person in front of you and you look up and thank whatever it was that warned you. Somebody's watching over you, and for that brief second, you remember that.

Or maybe it's late and you're shopping. You love to grocery shop at night because it's quiet and unhurried. The only people in the store are also night owls and the shared secret eye contact bonds you with your fellow shoppers. The music's better at night. You can buy tampons and Preparation H and who cares?

On this particular night you're taking your time; you're squeezing the Charmin and smelling the candles, when something in your head tells you to go check out.

You think to yourself, "Why?" You have no commitments, nothing's really on TV, and besides, you like the soft feeling of well-packed bathroom tissue. You dismiss this voice and finish up your shopping. You round the corner to the checkout area and there stands the only other person in the store, just starting to check out. And it appears she's preparing for the end of days. Her cart is filled, top to bottom, and even the bored cashier seems overwhelmed by the task. As you get closer, your eyes roll and your shoulders drop when you spy her "ask me about my grandchild" purse, which is bursting with coupons.

If you had listened to that voice two minutes ago, you'd be in your car and on your way back home. Now you're worried the milk you just got will expire before you even make it to your car.

Listening to that voice takes practice and trust, and if you're like me and you're really bad at both, it takes hard lessons to learn.

When I was sixteen, I quit high school and took my GED. We were dirt poor and I needed a job. I knew I could always get work at a restaurant because everybody needed to eat, so I decided to go to chef school. Because we were so poor, the state stepped in and paid for me to go to school. It was a godsend. So, for two years I went to chef school and worked as a cook in a couple different restaurants.

I was also in recovery; I sobered up when I was fourteen, but at the time, people my age in recovery were rare. In fact, only one other person my age was sober back then, so meetings were all full of people twice my age. It wasn't until I was sixteen that more and more people my age started going to treatment. This meant more people my age attending meetings, which meant I wasn't so alone in my recovery.

By the time I was in my late teens, the community was jumping with sober kids. I went to three meetings a week, went to chef school, and worked as a cook. That was my life for the latter part of my teens.

After two years, I graduated from chef school. But by then I was sick to death of cooking. Maybe if I had a little balance in my life vocation wise, I would have lasted longer. But the long hours, the crabby customers, and the diva chefs all took their toll on me. And the thought of cooking a hot dog seemed too much to bear. In that field you have to have passion, otherwise you burn out. I lacked that passion.

But I did have a passion for counseling. I loved going to meetings. I found I had a natural ability to talk to people. With my psychic abilities kicking in I could spot issues in a person a mile away. I was patient, I was strong, and I was gathering experience. I decided I wanted to work with adolescents in recovery.

With the influx of teens in recovery, more and more jobs were opening up for people my age with experience. Back then you didn't need a degree, you just needed a connection and some know-how. Some of my friends in AA had gotten jobs as counselors and they didn't have half the skills I thought I had. The money was better, you got to sit when you worked, and you didn't smell like grease at the end of the day.

But finding a job was hard. Everywhere I looked, I seemed to run into a roadblock. Meanwhile, my friends who sucked at counseling were doing amazing. They were buying new cars, wearing new clothes, and saving the world.

The owners of the restaurant I was working at decided to sell to a nail salon. I had a choice: go find another chef job or look full time for a counseling job. I knew I was supposed to be a counselor, so all my effort went into pursuing that.

Three months later I was out of money, I lost my apartment and my car, and I had to ask my mom if I could come live with her. She was overjoyed ... not.

She said I could only do it if I was out within a month. At the time, I felt I was so close to finding a counselor job that I knew I'd be fine, but a month came and went and there I was, still unemployed and sleeping on the couch.

Finally, she said I had to find another place to live; she was dating a guy and my being there was putting a damper on her love life. Plus I was almost twenty. I needed to go.

The only option I could think of was to live in a halfway house for sober youth. It was a long shot because I had been sober for a long time and generally they only let in people who were fresh out of treatment. Still, it was the only thing I could think to do.

Here's where that little voice came in; it screamed at me to be patient, to wait, just hang in a little longer. I was sure I would get a job, but time was running out, so I set up an interview at the halfway house.

When I got there I recognized some of the people from a meeting I regularly attended. It was humiliating because I was one of the few people my age with long sobriety. To make matters worse, the person running the place was none other than my old counselor, Betty.

For those who didn't read my first book, Betty is a no-nonsense, strong, powerful woman who can rip you to shreds with a look. She doesn't mince words, she doesn't fuck around, and she eats vulnerability with a spoon. You don't con Betty. As soon as I saw her, I knew I was screwed.

I walked into the interview and sat down. Beside Betty were four other people all in a circle, waiting to interview me. I looked around at the group and then at Betty, who was standing. She looked amazed.

"Michael," she said, "what the fuck are you doing here?" And just like the old days, I felt the blood rush to my head. I had rehearsed my monologue for a week. I worked on the right inflections and the proper pauses, but looking at Betty the only thing that came out was "aaaahhh well."

Mercifully, Betty let me off the hook. She dismissed the four interviewers, and when they shut the door she said, "Michael, you can't live here. Come on, you know that. You're embarrassing yourself." She then looked at me with a sick "I feel sorry for you" look and opened the door.

"Michael," she said, "get your shit together, will you?" and escorted me out the door.

You know when you don't think you can feel worse about something and then magically you find you can? That's how that day went.

The next two months were a struggle; I did a reading here and there, I worked part-time at a bakery, and I kept my eyes open for a possible counseling job. My mom eased up when she saw I was trying, but neither one of us wanted me there.

Finally, I caught a break. A dream job working with adolescents had opened up not far from my mom's. I fit the requirements, I had the experience, the money was amazing, and the hours were perfect. If I got the job, I'd be out of my mom's in no time, and there was no one with better experience. That job was mine.

But there was a drawback: it was for the same halfway house I had tried to become a resident at two months earlier. I had to convince Betty that I did what she told me to do: I had to come in looking like my shit was together, and that's exactly what I did. I borrowed a great suit from my buddy, I got new shoes, I fixed my hair—I was styling. This time when I walked in there, I walked with confidence, thinking "I'm a success story."

I walked in and the first thing Betty said was, "Michael, what the fuck are you doing here?" And again, my face felt flushed. In the two minutes it took Betty to explain how there was no way in hell she could hire me because just two months ago I was looking for a place to live, even my suit wanted to run away.

She added that if I hadn't come in two months ago and asked her if I could live there, she would have hired me on the spot. It felt like Jesus himself had kicked me in the balls.

I regretted not listening to that voice in my head for years because of that.

This story does have a good ending. I was so distraught that I started facilitating a group of teens at a treatment center for free. The head lady liked my style so much that they offered me a job at a detox center, which turned out to be one of my favorite jobs of all time. I moved out of my mom's and got a car.

So you would think after all of that I would always listen to that voice in my head and make my life easier, right? Well, you'd be wrong.

Not long after the Betty thing, a group of friends wanted to swim at this little island on the Mississippi River. The plan was to hang out all day, be by our lonesome, and jump off this big tire swing a friend of ours had put up a few days earlier.

Summer days in Minnesota can get hot and steamy, so anything concerning water, we liked.

The problem was getting there. The Mississippi River in Minneapolis can have strong currents, I think more so as it goes farther south, but sometimes the northern part of the city, where we were, isn't as turbulent. It can still be bad, people have died there. But for the most part it seems safer than it does in say, downtown or lower. When our buddy put up the tire swing, the current was calm; he said they found a sandbar and basically walked over to the island from the shore and put it up.

But the night before we came there was a huge thunderstorm and the river was definitely higher than it must have been for the tire guys. The current was visibly stronger, which meant the sandbar was probably underwater, so we were going to have to swim to the island.

None of this seemed dangerous in any way, because we were idiots. The thought of flying high on a tire swing clearly outweighed any possibilities of death or permanent injury; it was a beautiful day and nothing bad happens on beautiful days.

The island we wanted to get to was about a block downstream from where we were standing. In my mind I could jump in there and gently swim to the island, which seemed only about one hundred yards away. I wanted to go from there because I didn't want to walk along the riverbank looking for a submerged sandbar, with rats and wood ticks and mutant beavers just waiting to attack. I hate wood ticks.

Another reason I wanted to go from there was because something told me not to. I had a bad feeling—a really bad feeling—but I purposely wanted to prove to myself that it was okay.

My buddies weren't sure what to do. Bobo wanted to find the sandbar; he saw the current and thought the best thing to do was walk across, not swim. Steve was on the fence, and Bruno, a six-foot-tall, 250-pound rugby player, was ready to jump in with me. Bobo, who by this time was ten yards ahead, yelled that he thought he saw the sandbar. Hearing that, Bruno and Steve decided to follow Bobo. I told them I would see them in an hour when they got there and to watch out for river rats. Instantly Bruno started looking around like he saw something, and they disappeared through the long grass and shrubbery.

That weird "no" feeling was still with me when I jumped in and started swimming. Within the first ten seconds I knew I was in trouble. I looked up and I was twenty feet downriver from where I started, and only five feet from shore. I swam harder. As I neared the middle of the river I realized that something was also pulling me under; I was now fighting the current *and* whatever was pulling me down.

I swam as hard as I could, but the harder I swam, the more I was being pulled under. My arms were already tired, and as I felt this strong pull toward the bottom, down I went. I opened my eyes to try to get my bearings, but I couldn't even see my hands, all I saw was black. The water was becoming colder and colder the deeper I went down. I couldn't fight it, I was running out of air, and this wave of sheer panic ran through me. I knew I was a goner.

It was at that point that I heard a familiar female voice calmly say "relax." Nothing else, just a calm, clear voice: "relax." It felt like death itself was asking me to submit, and with no choices, I did what she said. I stopped fighting it, I let go. I felt a calmness come over me, a surrender. But as soon as I let go, I started floating toward the surface. It was like the force that had me just let me go.

But now I wasn't sure I would even make it to the surface. My lungs were burning and I had no fight left in me. And then I could feel the sun.

I took in the deepest breath I think I'd ever taken. I coughed, I gasped, and once again I struggled to gain control. Once again I heard the word "relax." I turned myself over and floated on my back. If the river took me to New Orleans, so be it. I could breathe, I was alive, and I could see the sky—that's all that seemed to matter. I floated on my back and kicked my way to the other side, my arms like lead balloons. I barely grabbed onto a branch that was hanging over the river and pulled myself onto the island. I walked back to where the tire swing was, collapsed in the sun, and waited for my friends to show up.

I was in shock: It was ninety degrees and I was shaking head to toe. It felt like every ounce of energy was taken out of my body and the fear of how I was going to get back filled me. But I was glad I was alone. I didn't want to talk about what happened, I didn't want my friends to see me shaking, and I sure as hell didn't want to use the damn tire swing.

Thirty minutes later when they finally came, I had stopped shaking and my body was warming up. Still, when I tried to move, my body felt heavy, sluggish. I laid there and pretended to be suntanning.

The rest of the afternoon was a blur. After trying out the swing and realizing the current was too strong, the boys reluctantly agreed we'd walk back via the sandbar, which was a great relief for me.

Now the skeptic might say that since I was raised around psychics, of course I would hear a voice at that time; it's what happens in my world. And an even more skeptical person might suggest that since I spent most of my early years on the water I might have been taught to relax in a situation like that and was just remembering. But that's not true.

In fact, I can say with 100 percent certainty that at no time did someone *ever* say to me, "Okay Michael, if you're in a river and the current pulls you down like the hands of death itself, just give up. Stop trying to swim and you'll be right as rain."

I didn't talk about that incident with anybody for a long time, not even my mom. Maybe I didn't want to admit to myself just how close I came to dying that day or maybe it felt self-inflicted and I didn't want to get yelled at. I knew I wasn't supposed to jump in when I did, I just didn't want to listen. Whatever the reason, I only told a couple of people in my life what happened. This is the first time I'm actually describing how it felt.

What if I told you a story about someone who listened to that voice and it saved her life?

One of my best buddies in the world recently started dating a girl he met online. We'll call her Jane. He was smitten. She's smart, attractive, and friendly, but has a story that I was surprised belonged to such a well-adjusted and normal person.

Jane said that when she was in her twenties she was walking to a friend's house one night when she noticed a man coming toward her on the same side of the street. She said she had a weird feeling when she looked at him, like she should cross the street and avoid him at all costs. But just like me when I was told not to jump in, she ignored that voice. She was half a block away from her friend's house and to go all the way around seemed stupid, so she kept on walking. When he passed her, she said she got this chill throughout her body, like he walked right through her. When she turned around to check on him, he was on her.

He grabbed her and wrestled her into the bushes off the street; they fought and tumbled. He hit her with a hammer and stabbed her in her side with a knife. She said she didn't even know she was bleeding because it had rained and they were both full of mud and water. She said he kept screaming at her to tell him her name.

During all of this she said she stayed calm, like she knew it was going to be okay. Jane kept hearing the name *Therese* in her head, so when he asked again, she told him her name was Therese. When she did, he stopped beating her.

"That's my sister's name," he said.

"My name is Therese," she said again, "just like your sister."

The beatings stopped, but the attack wasn't over. He raped her. But even during that, she said it was like she left her body and went and watched her mother and friend play cards. Later, when she was telling her mother about the ordeal, she described in detail what they were both wearing, the room they were in, and the details of the game.

This is not someone I would describe as a psychic. She's a woman who had a horrible experience and somehow trusted that voice, which, like me, saved her life.

The man would go on to assault another woman, but she wouldn't survive. He was eventually caught and went to prison. And it was Jane's contention that the gods chose her to be his victim that night, because anybody else he would have killed. She credits Spirit for telling her the name of her assailant's sister. She says that's what saved her life.

When she was a child, Jane used to practice leaving her body to visit her friends and family. When she looks back on that terrible night, she thinks to herself that it was as though she had been prepared, because she was able to detach herself from the emotional pain of what was happening to her. Because of that, she feels like more of a survivor, as opposed to a victim.

So, You Hear Voices. What Does That Have to Do with Answers?

It's the voice that helps us make decisions. Everyone has it. But so many of us block it out because we decide it's better to be logical than to trust it. We don't want to seem weak or stupid.

Psychics don't have to worry about looking stupid, because we're psychics! Some people already think we are stupid. But that helps us see what normal people don't always see.

You show me an X-ray and it just looks like a bunch of cloudy weirdness with bones here and there. Somebody who's trained to understand them sees everything. When they point to the issue, maybe you see it, maybe you don't, but if they're schooled, stuff just pops out for them and you trust their opinion. It's the same with psychics. We see the opportunities and the answers all the time. You might look at the same thing we see and not get it, but we do.

Some of us just smell like patchouli when we do it.

We get these little tools, instincts, intuition, gut feelings, whatever you want to call them, and they're supposed to help us figure stuff out.

And if we don't trust ourselves, we reach outside ourselves—to God, to the universe, whatever name you want to call it—and we beg and plead for answers. And when our questions seem to go unanswered, we blame God or feel unworthy or go to psychics.

This may come as a shock to some of you, but we are not the most evolved species in the universe. Personally, I think if there was a stupid planet, we'd be it. In so many readings I've done, I've come across souls who just hate it here. The way we treat each other, the drama, the backstabbing, the evil. It's a tough place to be.

We try so hard not to look stupid or be taken advantage of that we actually end up doing just that, because we don't trust ourselves. We want messiahs, teachers who know, people to follow.

But in every single reading I've ever done, each one of us has guides. And each and every time, those guides love the person they're around so deeply and believe in them so strongly. It's almost as though they see *us* as the person to follow.

And yes, they do try to show us answers, they try all the time. But we are friggin' mental. We go back and forth, we can't make decisions. How many times do you go to the McDonald's drive-through and have to sit and wait for the nimrod in front of you to decide what they want?

The menu hasn't changed in years! And there's a McDonald's every ten blocks. It's like people are looking at the menu for the very first time.

Can you imagine how frustrated your guides must be?

If you want answers, be clear on what you want. Don't just say "I want another job." What the hell other kind of job do you want?

You know what psychics hate the most? When people come in and say, "Oh, just tell me what you pick up on me." We pick up on *everything*. Should we start with your birth? Ask a specific question. Don't give details, just ask a direct question. Does Gertrude love me? Will I get the job? Will my pickle farming stock go up? Be clear on what you want.

And that is doubled when you ask your guides for help. Be clear, be specific. They want to help you, but how can they do that if you don't tell them what you want?

So many times, people come to me and say they keep asking and asking but nothing ever comes. They're mad because they feel forsaken. Alone in their quest for happiness. But when I ask them what they are looking for, they don't even know, they just want it to be better. How can your guides help you find your answers if you don't know the question?

I do readings for this lady in her mid-thirties who's an accountant. She hates her job. She hates the people she works with, she hates the office, she hates the hours. The girl is not happy.

She was making just good enough money to stop her from quitting. She had just bought a car so she needed to keep up with the payments, her condo wasn't exactly paid for, and she was single, feeling trapped and stuck. So day after day she went to work and day after day she was miserable.

As a last resort, she came to me. I don't get a lot of accountants; they tend to be logical types and psychics don't add up in their books. But this lady was so desperate she had to try something.

I tend to be direct in my readings. I've beaten around too many bushes in my time, so I figure, screw it.

"You're supposed to write children's books," I said, because that's all her guides would tell me. Oh, they told me about her life and who she was and all that crap, but as far as her future, that's all they wanted to say.

And they said it in a way that made me think they had told her before, like they were tired of telling her. They did say it was important that she at least follow that path. And they were going to try to show her how important it was. They said her current job was really stupid, and that she knew that but she lacked the trust to do what she really wanted to do.

When I was finished talking, she looked at me in amazement. She said she had always wanted to write children's books but had no idea how to go about it. And now she was stuck in her career. How could she possibly start doing that? I told her I'm sure she didn't know how to be an accountant in the beginning, but somehow she figured that out. Maybe she could at least try to figure out how to go about it.

My suggestion only seemed to upset her, being the practical accountant that she was. She couldn't figure out how she was going to manage it all. Personally, it seemed pretty obvious to me: write a book, scribble a sentence, do something, but don't just sit there and look lost.

Two weeks after she left, I got a text. She had been let go from her job and she was panicked. What in the world was she going to do now?

I replied: Write a book. She never responded.

A year later I got a package. Inside was a purple children's book by an author I didn't recognize and a note: "Please thank my dead friends for me, and thank you for the reading." She signed her real name.

Her little voice had told her to write a book, her guides just helped give her the time to do it. That happens all the time.

If you want answers you need to have an idea of what you really want. Don't wait for a sign that it's the right decision. If you really want something, start the process. I promise they will help.

It's as simple as sending a letter.

First, you get clear on who you want the letter to go to. Then you write it. That takes action on your part, "they" need action. The only way they can help you is when you do some action.

Then you address the letter. That means you're clear on what you want. You can't just send a letter without an address, you have to know where you want it to go. That means you need intent.

Now you bring the letter to the mailbox. That means action: you take action, you have intent. Now Spirit really can help.

The last and hardest thing you do is you let go of the letter and put it into the box. This step is the most important. You don't hold on to the letter, you don't squeeze it and hope somehow it gets delivered, you let it go and you *know* it will get delivered.

Most people won't do the last step. They try to control the letter. They can't trust and let go. When you know the letter will get delivered, it changes things.

Spirit will help you as much as they can during this process, but when they really shine is when you trust in your heart and let that letter go.

Action and intent: listening to that voice and KNOW- ING it will happen. Not hoping, knowing.

It starts with that voice. If you do hear that voice, just listen, even if you're tired, even if you're beat, even if you've had a long day and you just want to hang out at home, watch a mindless show, and not think.

Listen to that voice telling you to go see your mom. You love your mom and you wouldn't mind seeing her because it's been forever since you have, and you probably should. But it's twenty miles away, traffic at this time is a bitch, and honestly, the old folks home gives you the creeps.

You say this to yourself as you put your coat on and look for your keys. You know that voice, you know the difference between "be a good son" voice and "do what I say" voice. There's a difference in tone, in weight. So you pay attention and you go.

And when you finally get there you're glad you came. You go to the McDonald's across the street and get her favorite, chicken nuggets and orange pop. You make your way past the walking zombies, who are now awakened by the smell of food, and you find refuge in the slowest elevator this side of the Mississippi.

When you get to her door, you knock, but you let yourself in because you know it would literally kill her to come to the door herself. You walk in, say hello, and there on the couch sits this tiny sweet woman you know as your mother, with an ear-to-ear grin, so happy to see you. Now you are very glad you came.

Like a little girl at Christmas, her eyes get big when you show her the food you brought her. She asks you what it is, and when you tell her, she seems shocked you knew exactly what to get her, even though you get her the same thing every time you visit.

You settle in and watch her favorite shows, you barely talk.

You look over at her from time to time and you catch her just staring at you, so you go sit next to her and put her little head on your shoulder. That seems better. And the night goes by slowly. Maybe you tell her you love her and she squeezes your hand. You might even say you're going to miss her when she goes, but you don't really want to go there because you didn't come there to say goodbye. Instead you say something like "Boy, we went through a lot together didn't we?"

And she looks up at you and says, "Yes we did, but we had each other." And for a second you feel that sadness well up in you, but when you look in her eyes, you see a thousand layers of love, so you put her head back on your shoulder and smile instead of cry.

It's late and it's time to go; you don't want to leave, but you can't really stay. She's tired, and you know this by her immediate response when you suggest you should probably go. "Okay honey," she says before you can finish your last word, "I'll see you tomorrow."

You stand to go, but just as you do, she seems to wake up. She has a list of instructions she must tell you before she forgets. She starts to tell you who, what, and where, but then relaxes when she sees you looking at her with a smile. "It's okay, Mom," you tell her, "I'll see you in the next couple of days."

You hug her gently, you tell her you love her, and you go.

When you close the door, you look back and see her smiling at you and you wonder, like you always do, if this is the last time you'll see her.

Two days later, on a Friday, you get a call from your oldest sister in a voice you've never heard from her, saying, "She's gone, Michael, Mom passed." And even though you knew this day would come and maybe a small part of you is relieved, you feel shocked that it's actually real.

As you pull yourself together and get ready to go see her again for truly the last time, you think back to that voice and you think how lucky you are to have it, and how glad you are that you listened. Because knowing you had that one last night together will make the days and weeks to come more bearable.

Dead Guides Talking

So, let's talk about guides.

The theory is that we all have guides around us that help and learn from us. Some people call them guardian angels, some call them angels. I call them guides, because to me, that's what they are.

In my opinion, there is a difference between spirit guides and guardian angels. To me, guardian angels are big; they are much more evolved than your average spirit guides. They're like the bosses, the overseers.

Spirit guides are more likely souls who will come back. They learn from us, they observe, they try to help. You'll feel them more because they seem closer to us.

I saw my first guide when I was around eight years old. A lady had come to the house for a reading with my mom.

I was used to people coming in and out of our house, so her being there wasn't that big of a deal. But what caught my attention was the posse she walked in with. She had three or four "souls" accompanying her. And none of them looked like any spook I'd ever seen.

Even at that tender age I had seen my share of spirits. Each one had a different light around them, usually white or off-white, some even darker. And they all came in different shapes and sizes.

I didn't like seeing ghosts, they gave me the creeps, but at my house they came with the dinner. Literally.

But the people that came with this lady were different. They weren't creepy, like regular ghosts were; they seemed kind and loving. And their color was different, gold and silver looking.

When she came into the kitchen where I was, they seemed to fill the room. Each one had this glow to it, which resonated from its core.

They saw that I could see them and they all smiled, like someone would when they were genuinely glad to see you. I looked around to see if others in the room could also see what I was seeing, but judging by their lack of awe I assumed they couldn't.

This struck me as odd, because these people were so amazing. My best choice was to chalk it up to my imagination; I had a good one back then and I didn't mind seeing things that weren't really there. Still, they really did feel real.

Before my mother started her reading I took her aside and told her what I saw. Instead of shooing me away, she asked me to describe to her what I saw, so I did. They were so clear and bright that it was easy to do, right down to the color of their eyes.

She asked the women if any of the people I described sounded familiar to her, like maybe I was showing that I had medium skills. But the woman shook her head and said none of them sounded familiar. So I let it go.

About a week after I saw her, the lady came back for another reading. She told my mom she gave some thought to what I said and what I described. She said she was certain that they weren't people she knew that had passed, but my description of them seemed familiar to her. She said for some reason she felt comforted that I saw them around her.

Nobody really knew what to think of it; it was just another weird thing that happened at the house, but it did make me feel better that she was comforted. At least nobody made fun of me or took me away to a nice, quiet room.

As time went on, I saw these "souls" with the gold and silver lighting around them more frequently.

And I didn't just see them when I was practicing readings. I'd see them when I was talking to my friends, my siblings, and even my teachers at school.

I was in gym class one time and Mr. Wood, our gym teacher, was trying to teach me the fine art of a proper burpee.

Mr. Wood hated me. He thought I threw a giant snowball at his favorite student, a girl named Jessica, and knocked her down. Sure, I had been known to throw a snowball or two, but those were at friends and moving cars. I didn't know Jessica well enough to throw a snowball at her, but I liked her; she was sweet. The guy who did throw the snowball was a guy named Snot-Nosed Billy. He knew Jessica, and when I arrived on the scene, I saw him throw the snowball and run away. I was helping her up after he knocked her down, when Mr. Wood rounded the corner and saw her covered in snow with me standing over her. Wrong place, wrong time.

I wasn't about to turn in Snot-Nosed Billy, because I really didn't think Mr. Wood would believe me, plus he was nowhere to be seen. The scene looked pretty cut and dry. And I didn't mind that Mr. Wood thought what he thought, because Jessica knew it wasn't me and that was all that mattered. But since that time, he had it in for me.

So there I was doing burpees for God knows what reason this time, and I look over at Mr. Wood and see those people around him, the ones with the gold and silver colors. There were three of them, and just by looking at them I could tell they really loved Mr. Wood.

It was the polar opposite of how I was feeling at the time.

You have to understand that in my mind Mr. Wood was a tyrant—a pushy, mean, cold son of Satan who had no redeeming qualities except the ability to make me look stupid. He didn't care about me and never showed me any real kindness, but watching these beings act so loving toward Beelzebub Jr. had me confused, to say the least. Why would these souls care so much about a complete dick?

But just as I was wondering that, these people started showing me a different side of who Mr. Wood really was.

I could see them looking at me and then at Mr. Wood. They adored him; they looked like they would do anything for this man if they could. But they could also see that I was puzzled, conflicted. One of them looked directly at me, and for a moment it felt like I was seeing Mr. Wood through their eyes.

I saw how hard he worked for his family, I saw his disappointment at how his life turned out. I saw how he wished he could have provided more for them. How kind he actually was, how noble he actually was. I saw his daughters. I didn't think the man could get a date, let alone a wife and kids. But I saw how they looked up to him, how gentle he was, protective.

I couldn't help but feel compassion for the man after that. I actually started to admire him.

I snapped out of my love fest with his guides when Mr. Woods caught me staring his way. With his veins popping out and his tongue on fire, he asked me rather loudly what I was staring at. Rather than tell him the truth and introduce him to his guides, I panicked and said, "Umm your face," which was true. When he asked me again, this time with added vigor and spit, I thought it was a trick question, so I stuck to my original answer.

It was a lot of pressure on a young lad with HCICSG (holy crap I can see guides) syndrome. I really didn't know what to say. I knew I couldn't tell him what I just learned; I'd be chopped into little pieces and thrown into the loony bin—or worse, detention—but I didn't want him to think poorly of me. So I shut up, a rarity for me.

Mercifully, he only made me sweep the gym floor with a paint brush, but it didn't matter. I felt like I knew the real guy now, underneath the rotten, crusted, "drop and give me twenty" asshole I had come to know. He wasn't that guy; he was trying to figure it out just like everybody else. After that day I liked him.

I still didn't really know who those souls were, or what they wanted. They were all different, nobody was the same, but they all had that odd light to them.

I was happy with assuming it was my imagination. So many people were trying to single themselves out as unique, show that they were different (meaning better than the rest), and I didn't want to enter the fray with stories of glowing people, so I kept it mostly to myself.

It wasn't until my late teens, when I started doing professional readings, that these "people" started to make sense to me.

My preference was to do the opposite of what I saw growing up. The last thing I wanted was to be in a quiet room with thick drapes and creepy lighting. I needed loud and busy. I wanted the feel of the conversations I was having to be as normal as having lunch with a friend. So I met people for lunch.

This particular day I was doing a reading for a lady named Clare, a friend of my mother's, at a busy delicatessen during the noon rush.

When she came in, it looked like she came in with three other people, only the other three had that light around them. My first reaction was frustration. I didn't want to read four people, I didn't want to be judged or watched by other people when I did readings. But as she got closer, I realized the other three didn't have feet. Still, they were so vivid that I had to mention them to Clare.

I said hello and asked how she was; she seemed nice. But then I asked her if any of the people I saw sitting next to her were her relatives or friends. I knew I wasn't supposed to ask questions like that; I was supposed to know who those people were, but these weren't like the normal dead people your average Joe psychic sees.

I described what they looked like and a smile came across her face.

"Those are my guides," she said, "your mother said you'd be able to see them. Can you tell me about them?"

I paused. "Guides?" I asked, "What the hell is a guide?"

If this had been a driver's test the instructor would have kicked me out of the car and suggested I take the bus.

There are only a few things you're supposed to do when you do readings, but I was doing all the things you're not supposed to do. Honestly, I didn't know that I cared. I was seeing these people all over the place and now there was a lady coming to me for a reading and she seemed to know more about them than I did. I was already looking like a complete amateur and I probably wasn't going to get paid, which meant I shouldn't order that corned beef, coleslaw, and French dressing sandwich that I really liked, because I didn't bring any money.

"Well," she said patiently, "from what I understand from Birdie, they are our guardian angels."

Birdie was our teacher, my psychic mentor. She loved my sister and mother and tolerated me because she saw that I had abilities. I was always at odds with Birdie because I wasn't comfortable with my gifts or the psychic world as a whole, so I always felt she was testing me, trying to get me to conform. I admired her for her strengths, even feared her because of them. She was the strongest psychic I had ever known, but I bucked her instructions as much as I could— my way of fighting the man.

Now my head was buzzing. Was this a test from Birdie, was Clare a mole? How did she know Birdie and why didn't Birdie tell *me* about guides?

And could I at least borrow the money for that sandwich?

And then it hit me. Birdie *did* tell me about guides, but when she said guardian angels, I envisioned people with wings and harps. I didn't think that meant normal looking people.

I started to think. When I saw these figures, they were always around other people, like Mr. Wood or people who came to get readings. Unlike normal dead people, these beings didn't talk; they thought their words. Even then, it wasn't just words; it was like they put you right in the person's heart. It was simple yet complex, deep and light all at the same time. They were much more loving and more full than your average Casper, and their light was very different than Spirit.

I gathered myself and looked again at her guides, with the pressure of wondering if these were relatives or friends gone. I didn't have to concentrate on the stupid stuff like whether they smoked or what dress they wore at their funeral. I could just listen to what they had to say. If it made sense, great; if not, maybe it would later on.

Her guides were patient with me as I stumbled to figure out who they were.

When I settled in they began to "talk" to me and with my worry filter gone, the words just flowed. I couldn't get them out fast enough, and now more than one of them was talking. I stopped and asked if she had any paper and pen to write some of their thoughts down, but all she had was a pen. I grabbed a napkin and started writing all the things they were saying, or at least the main points of what they were saying.

I didn't even look at her while I was doing this. I just kept writing and talking.

When they stopped talking, I stopped too, and I looked up to see if she was still there. She was, and she was crying. At first I wasn't sure if it was because I said the wrong thing or if she was upset because she wasted her day on a semi-slow psychic. I asked her if she was okay and she shook her head yes. I asked if she needed me to explain what I just said and she shook her head no.

She sat in silence until finally she looked up at me and said thank you. She said she was blown away by the information and needed some time to process it. She asked if I would mind if she left. I said, "No, of course not."

She stood up, pulled a fifty from her purse and said, "Here, thank you."

I stood up, gave her a hug, and thanked her for the money. I reminded her that the cost was only twenty-five, but she insisted I take the fifty. She paused again like she was going to ask me a question, but then shook her head and again thanked me.

Wow, I thought to myself. Fifty bucks!

I still wasn't sure about the guide thing. I understood that it made sense for Clare, and I understood the principle behind what they might be. These were different beings. But—and I mean no disrespect to the woo-woos out there—most of the people in the psychic community, or at least those that hung out at my house, would believe just about anything. You could tell them a unicorn was doing a jig behind them and they'd turn around and say, "Oh yeah, I see it."

But I did feel better about my readings regardless of who these beings were, because the information came so clearly.

And as I did more readings, these "guides" became clearer. I was growing more comfortable with them and it seemed they were more comfortable with me. Every once in a while, someone would ask me where I was getting my information. If it felt right I would tell them I saw people around them, and they were giving me the information. More and more people were commenting on how they had also seen these people around them, so the idea was becoming less and less crazy.

And then this happened.

I started doing a reading for a nice, quiet guy I'd never met before. Normally when I do a reading, guides just show up and start telling me stuff, sometimes three or four at a time, so I have to try to pick apart what each of them is saying. It's good that they're talking, but a pain to figure it out. Anyway, this guy sat down, I sat down. I was waiting for someone to show up and start talking and I got nothing but crickets. I thought maybe I wasn't supposed to give this guy a reading, which happens from time to time.

But I could feel guides around him. Like when you're lying down with your eyes closed and you can feel someone come into the room.

Now I was confused. Were these souls going to talk to me or not? And if not, what the hell were they doing in the restaurant?

I asked them, not out loud but more to myself, like "Hello, anybody home?" Then I saw these alien-looking creatures standing over this guy, kind of smiling. I say *kind of* because they weren't like smiling like you and I smile, but I could just tell they were happy. Their eyes were huge, their mouths were tiny, and they were really tall. They didn't have a hair on them and very little muscle structure, but they felt powerful. They also oozed love and pride for this guy, like he was one of them.

I had heard stories of people from other planets coming here to learn since I was a tadpole, so it wasn't a complete shock, but it was still a pretty good shock.

They didn't talk, but I could hear them clearly. It was like speech got in the way; they could communicate words and emotions at the same time. I could feel their love and concern for this guy all at once. It was a pretty amazing experience. After the initial shock wore off, I found it easier to communicate with these beings than with humans.

They told me all about him, how he felt so alone and detached from humans, how he struggled to fit in, and that he was tired of trying. They went on and on about what his mission was and how he could achieve it. They wanted me to reassure him that he wasn't alone and suggested a way to open the conversation. They said all these things within seconds of their appearance and I was amazed at how efficient they were at communication.

I had to smile and laugh at myself. I had finally gone over the edge. Soon I'd be eating apple sauce with a safe spoon at a quiet rest place for insane psychics. "I blame my mother," I thought. "No way can I tell this guy he's an alien."

Most people get a little iffy just meeting me for lunch. Telling them they might be from the Planet X doesn't instill serenity. I checked back with the ETs but, as sweet as they were, they didn't seem obliged to hold my hand, so on I went.

I looked at the man, who was fidgety by now, and apologized for taking so long, though in reality it was only a matter of minutes. I did what they said and told him that I knew he looked at the stars and missed home. When I did, his eyes filled up and he began to cry. "Thank God," I thought to myself, "I don't have to be locked up and wear pajamas for six months." We began the reading.

This wouldn't be the last time I saw "alien" spirit guides around people; in fact it started happening more and more as I got used to the idea. But still, it was odd to see these beings around people. Most of the time the people they were around seemed relieved when I told them about their guides, like it made sense to them.

Guides, no matter where they come from, seem to love us deeply. They only want us to succeed and be happy.

I can just hear the skeptics: "Is this one of those Tinker Bell, 'I believe' type deals?" No, it's not. Guides are around us whether you believe in them or not. Ask them to show you! That's what our old teachers taught us. Ask for a sign. You can, it's part of the deal.

My mother used to put a piece of paper and a pencil by her bed at night and ask them to write something down. Sometimes it would take days until she got something, but she always did. This was before we learned about earthbound spirits and how they wanted our attention, so it was more than likely something from them rather than a guide, but still, my mom got excited.

What you *can* ask for is guidance, but for God's sake, be clear on what you want.

If you tell your guides you want to be happier, you're in for the ride of your life.

A woman I've done readings for for years came to me pissed off because in part of the reading I told her to ask her guides to show her happiness. I did warn her that the path isn't always what we want it to be, but she didn't hear that part.

She said shortly after asking her guides, she started seeing all the people in her life who were bad for her. Then they showed her how empty and hard her job was. Then she said money problems started happening. They were doing cutbacks at her work and rather than be let go she agreed to a pay cut, but she still worked the same hours.

Then her moods started to change. She lost her patience with people, she started to get weepy at odd times, frustrated, anxious. So when she came back to me, she was ready to ask for a refund. Not only did she not get the answers she was looking for, but since she asked, life had gotten considerably worse.

But, here's what she didn't see. Every one of those things *was* an answer. The people they showed her *were* bringing her down and wearing her out. The job she was at *did* suck, it wasn't the right place for her at all. And of course the money sucked; if the money was great, she'd be less likely to leave. This way she was much more able to walk away if she wanted to.

As I explained this to her, her expression turned from "fuck you" to "hmm...okay." I continued.

I told her the mood swings she was having were helping her make decisions. She was no longer bound by what she thought other people would think was right, because now she was thinking for herself.

I told her she was ready. She was clear-headed, she was pissed off, but she was willing to step through the doors she wasn't able to in the past.

She seemed to get it.

She gathered her things and we walked toward the door. I hugged her goodbye, and as she walked out the door

I quickly mentioned that she would probably get fired in the next week or so, but not to worry because it was all a part of the plan. Sometimes I like to wait until the last minute to share things like that, so I don't have to deal with the aftermath.

The last thing I heard was, "Wait...*what?*" Until a month later when she confirmed that she did indeed get fired. But the story does have a happy ending. She was scared for a week or two, but then started looking. She applied for a job that a year ago she would have never applied for. But because she was so pissed, she thought why not.

She was calling me to tell me she got the job, and she was really excited to start her new life.

All of this wasn't my doing, it was hers. She put herself in the position to change, which her guides helped her do, just not in the way she was hoping they would.

This also works for you negative types too. If you're the kind of person who only sees shitty things with shitty people and shitty jobs, guides can accommodate you as well. In fact, it's way easier.

If you think you're too stupid to be in the job you want, they'll help you find a stupid job. If you feel more comfortable around asshole people, they'll surround you with asshole people. If you complain and complain, they'll help you find things to complain about. They don't judge, they just want you happy. If you're happy being miserable, consider it done. All your dreams will come true.

It's not a punishment, it's just simple reasoning.

That's the thing about guides: you ask them for something and it's always a surprise how they answer it for you.

You ask for patience, they park you behind a lady going twenty on the freeway. You ask for money and you find a five in your pocket. You ask for a lot of money, you get a check in the mail from someone who owed it to you, which happens to be the same amount you owe someone else. You ask for unconditional love, you find a lost puppy.

Everything is about learning.

A guy I like, Mike, came to me for a reading a few years ago and his only questions were about whether he was going to be a cop. He'd been a security guy for years but he really wanted to be a cop.

His guides agreed; they felt he was supposed to be a cop. But everything they were getting from him said he just wanted to stay a security guy. He wasn't applying for schools, he wasn't checking out leads, he was just talking to people about how great it would be to be a cop.

When I told Mike what they said, he came back with more excuses than a politician. The schools he liked didn't accept him, money was too tight, he didn't want to work in Florida. On and on this guy went with reasons why he couldn't be a cop.

Finally, I told him to just stay a security guy and see what comes up. Needless to say, I didn't get a tip.

I ran into Mike a few weeks back. He's still a good guy and he's still a security guard, but the ironic thing is that most of the time he works side by side with real cops. As he's gotten to know some of them he's found out that a lot of them had worse qualifications than he did. Some really struggled getting into school, some had to go to out of state to get work. All the excuses he gave me, these people had faced, but they kept going.

So he was surrounded by living reminders of what he wanted to become and should have become. Some of them even said to him, "Too bad you didn't want to be a cop, Mikey. You'd be a good one."

Guides can't make you do anything, but I know they try.

The old psychics believed that the reason you got the new car or new job or relationship you wanted was because that was the car, the job, or the person you were supposed to get.

Meaning they knew you were going to need a new car and they knew a Mustang in your price range was going to be available. The old psychics believed Spirit would make you want a Mustang, so you would look for one and voilà!, there it was.

This theory always confused the hell out of me, because it seems like it has a lot of holes in it, but what it boils down to is that sometimes we want certain things *because* we are going to get those things.

Yes, I know the doehays out there are thinking, "Well what if I want a million dollars? Ha ha!"

Well, there have been a ton of people who had that desire, and a lot of them have seen it come true. There's story after story of people writing checks to themselves and later being able to cash them.

But there are also tons of stories like Mike's. You chose which way you want to go.

Guides aren't genies, they don't grant wishes. But they do help you obtain yours.

DEATH OF A SALESMAN, A STRANGER, AND A FRIEND

People ask me a lot of questions about a lot of things, but the biggest question I get is about death. What happens when you die? Is there a heaven or hell?

In all the conversations I've had with my elders about dying, I was told that when you died and crossed into the light, God (or whatever you call it) would be there to meet you and review your life.

I was told this is what people referred to as hell: being in the presence of this amazing, powerful, loving being and reviewing all of your bad decisions, missed opportunities, and selfish acts.

If this is true, I hope they let you shut your eyes.

I'd like to believe there's a heaven. I'd like to believe we have choices on where to go next. But I don't think I'll truly know until I pass.

What I do know is that your soul does leave your body when you pass. And I do know most souls don't stay here when they die. I also know there's a different place they go when they die. I also know that wherever it is, people are happy there.

I know this because I've seen it.

I deal with death a lot in my job—I talk to dead people, I see dead people, I hear stories about dead people, and I try to find dead people. In fact, I think it's fair to say I deal with death more than your average undertaker, unless of course your average undertaker happens to be a psychic too. But I've also been around a lot of physical death. I've lost friends and family, as we all have, but I've been witness to more than a few people passing. Each time I've seen this, it's impacted me and changed the way I view life. I want to tell you about a few.

The moment right before someone I love dies, the world stops. The pulse of the city, the movement of the world, even my breath is suspended until I feel the soul leave the body and pass to the other side. And in that moment, I feel as close to them and to God as humanly possible for someone still alive. Such was the case with my friend Denny.

The Salesman

It's not easy to describe Denny because he wore so many hats. The quickest way would be to say he was a six-foot leprechaun. A comic friend of ours, Louie Anderson, introduced us to each other back in the mid-eighties. This was probably the best thing Louie ever did for me. We were at a function Louie was hosting and he thought Denny and I might get along. He was right.

Apparently, Denny had heard from either Louie or somebody else that I was a psychic, because the first thing he said to me after "hello" was the typical stupid question *everybody* who doesn't have a clue asks a psychic.

"So, what's in my future?"

"I'm not sure you have a future. Get a blood test," I replied.

That's when I usually walk away leaving the person wondering if I was serious or not. But Denny was different. He had a smile that was a cross between pure joy and the devil, and just watching this guy's reaction made me like him. We both laughed at what I'd said and I reassured him he wasn't going to die. He seemed relieved.

We got to talking about people we knew and things we did and as it often does, it turned out we had a lot in common. We were both in recovery and we knew a lot of the same people. He had heard about my family, I had heard about my family. It seemed like we had traveled the same road, but somehow managed to just miss each other. By the end of our short conversation, he booked a reading.

As I mentioned earlier, I used to do readings in bars or restaurants, anywhere that was loud and full of people. (I wasn't in love with the idea of being a psychic, so if I had to do them, I was going to do readings on my terms and where I wanted to be.) My clients, on the other hand, didn't know what to think about meeting at Al's Bar for a reading. But if they didn't want to go I figured I didn't have to do the reading, so I saw it as a win-win.

I asked Denny if he had a favorite place to meet and he suggested the Voodoo Room—a hip downtown bar that was known for being a bit wild. "Okay, perfect," I thought.

I don't remember exactly what we talked about during that first reading, but I do remember that I liked him— something I rarely felt after I did readings for people. And I know he liked what I said, because for most of it he was speechless. He just kept shaking his head and asking me how I knew this shit. This was Denny's first reading, so it was like a magic trick for him. Whatever it was, Denny was hooked. We talked for a long time that first day, and the more we talked, the more I liked him.

We started hanging out socially. Denny knew everybody and everybody knew him—he was salesman, and he was a good one. He was funny, charming, slippery, and devilish. If you didn't want what he was selling, you did by the end of the conversation. Maybe a week or two later you'd think, "What the hell? I didn't want another cheese straightener." But at the time, you'd buy a dozen. That was Denny. He just had that *thing* about him.

One of my favorite Denny stories was when he was a producer for a small-budget independent movie. Money was tight and there were no real stars in the movie. The movie was being made by a first-time director and being shot locally in Minneapolis, which was not exactly the recipe for an influx of cash. But Denny believed in this movie, so he worked everybody he knew to try to fund it. Big money, small money, it didn't matter.

One day, they were hours away from shutting down the project because the money was gone. They couldn't make the payroll and people were getting edgy about continuing the film. Denny secured a loan from a private investor in the nick of time to keep it going. But on the way to Denny's office, with the check in hand, the investor was involved in a serious car crash and was rushed to the hospital. It appeared all was lost—they'd had so many setbacks (natural disasters, fighting between the cast and crew) that this latest issue just seemed to be the nail in the coffin. But Denny kept going. He grabbed his coat, ran to the hospital, and somehow, as the investor was going into surgery, got the check from him to save the day.

When he came back from the hospital, people asked him if the investor was okay or if Denny was okay. All he said, with that grin only Denny had, was, "Doesn't matter. I got the check."

Now some would say he was heartless. (In fact, if you asked the investor's family, that would have been the nicest thing they'd say.) But the people who depended on Denny were in awe. If he believed in that film so strongly, they could put aside their petty differences and get behind it too. And they did. They finished the film.

The other side of Denny was that he could be a little untruthful. He meant well and his heart was in the right place, but his words didn't always meet his actions. Like the time at my wedding when he announced that he was sending us to Mexico for our honeymoon. That never happened. Or the time he was going to hire me to work with his new company and make millions? He forgot. Or the membership to the swanky health club I was going to get for doing readings with him, which never came to fruition. Or all the people he was going to introduce me to who could have opened huge doors for me—just didn't happen. And the amazing thing about Denny was that he could set it up so *you'd* feel bad if something he said didn't come true. He would apologize so deeply you'd have to go to counseling to deal with your guilt.

Needless to say, he went through people and friends with ease, but we always kept in touch.

And then one day he was walking around the lake and suddenly started bleeding from everywhere—nose, mouth—everywhere. They rushed him to the hospital and managed to barely save his life, but the news wasn't good.

He found out he had hepatitis C, he was a diabetic, and his liver was failing. If he didn't get a liver transplant soon, he was going to die. News spread like wildfire that Denny was sick, and everybody was in shock. He had been sober for years, didn't smoke, stayed in shape, and wasn't a big eater. He was Denny. Denny types don't die—you may want to kill them, but Dennys don't die.

Turns out it wasn't his time—his nephew donated half of his liver and saved Denny's life. The world wasn't ready for Denny to die and neither was he. He came back with that lucky charm attitude and decided to do something great with his life. During this whole ordeal, what amazed me was his calmness. He didn't act afraid, he just tackled the next challenge. While I would have been in the fetal position asking for my mother and a diaper change, Denny didn't do that. He kept going. You see a person's true character under situations like that, and he handled it well.

We got close again after that—golfing when we could, watching the fights when they were on, and talking about his new joy, making documentaries about organ transplants.

Life seemed to be going well for Denny and it was fun hanging out with him again.

One day he came to the house for a reading and he looked great. He was happy and excited and had just completed a little film about the organ transplant thing. He was also hoping to meet another girl. (I purposely left out the stories of Denny and his women because that could truly fill a whole different book, but it's safe to say he did love the ladies.) But among the million questions he did ask that day was one about a little lump under the skin on his forearm. He was worried it might be a big deal because his doctor seemed concerned when Denny described it to him on the phone.

He had made an appointment to have it checked the next day, but wanted my opinion on whether he should worry or not. I tuned into him and the first impression I got was of all these buds under his skin that felt like they were going to explode. They were all over his body. I told him this and we both just thought it was weird. He asked me repeatedly if he was okay and I just kept saying, "Yes, don't worry it's not a big deal," but in my mind I thought, "Holy crap, this feels bad, really bad."

He went to the doctor the next day and found out it was cancer. He called me immediately and asked if he was going to be okay. I said, "Yes, don't worry, it's okay." But I knew it wasn't. I couldn't deal with the real possibility of Denny dying, so I lied. I had never done that before, but I knew if I said, "Yes, you're sick," it would be real, and I couldn't fathom Denny being gone. I just couldn't.

They did an MRI on his whole body and found the cancer was in his liver, his brain, his pancreas, *everywhere*! Within two weeks of our visit, Denny was at death's door. With all that he had gone through, all that he had overcome, and who he was to me, I couldn't come to grips with it. I knew I had let him down. I didn't fully understand why

I wasn't honest with him. I felt like a coward, and I was ashamed to see him. His friend asked me to please come say goodbye, so I went. I sat with him and the many people who came to say their goodbyes. When he saw me he smiled and said, "So, is it still going to be okay?" I smiled back and said, "Blow me!"—an expression we used with each other almost daily. His eyes were shut, but that smile was still strong.

"I love you, Mikey," he said. "I'm so glad you're here."

My eyes started to well up.

"I love you too, Denny," I replied and his smile faded as he went in and out of consciousness.

The amazing thing about death is the transformation. On nights such as this when the person is dying gracefully and they're surrounded by the people they love, that love fills the room. And as it progresses, the death angels come into the room. They are magnificent beings—huge angels filled with love and compassion. Their only purpose is to transport the souls to the other side, and they do it with great care.

Right before Denny died, I could see them coming. They bring a hushed tone and calming effect to the room. Sometimes the lighting in the room changes, as it did that night, and you no longer feel sad or alone. You feel like it's okay to let go; you know you will see them again. That's what happened the night my friend Denny the salesman died.

The Twin

Not long before I started my book, I had an interesting experience. I was struggling a bit on whether or not to even write another book because it was never my dream to be a writer, and in my mind I was far from being one. But I had a lot of stories to tell and these stories all seemed to fit under the same umbrella—answers.

So, on my way home from shopping I was told by that voice inside to go back to the store I had just come from. Being a psychic and having heard that voice a thousand times I knew ignoring it wasn't an option—like when your mother tells you to come to dinner for the fourth time and you know the consequence of a fifth time is long, slow, painful death, so you go.

So I went back into the belly of the beast in rush hour traffic. I wasn't sure what I needed or forgot at the store, but I just knew I had to go.

As I got close, I heard emergency vehicles coming up from behind me—ambulances, police, fire trucks all bearing down. I pulled over to let them pass and I noticed they were all going to the same store I was going to.

As I pulled into the lot, I noticed the emergency people were all centered around an older gentleman just outside the main door. One of the EMTs was frantically performing CPR on the man, and when I parked my car and walked closer to the scene, I could see it wasn't working. I've never been an ambulance driver or worked in the ER, but I've been around death enough to know when someone is a goner, and this man appeared to be dead.

He looked to be in his late fifties or early sixties, with slightly grey hair, and was casually dressed, lying flat on his back. His arms were spread wide apart as if he were on a cross and his skin had that purplish off-white color—the color someone has when they've passed or are about to.

A crowd had gathered to watch the efforts by the paramedics. Other than the occasional gasp when a new person would arrive to witness the scene, nobody was making a sound. Another clue that this was more serious than just an injured man lying on the ground was the color of the scene, the actual hue. It was dusk, so the light was changing from light blue to dark blue. The emergency lights were getting brighter as the night got darker, and the cold crisp air seemed to hold everything in slow motion. But there's this particular light that comes with death—a kind of energy that's only there when someone's going to pass. I'd seen it a couple times at accident scenes and once at a robbery where a guy got killed. It's like a bright white undertone. It's actually really beautiful.

As I looked around and observed the crowd, I noticed a man kneeling and staring, dressed exactly like the man lying on the ground. He had his hand over his mouth as if he were in shock, a look of complete panic on his face. His level of grief seemed overwhelming and I felt bad, because at first I assumed it was the dead man's twin. They both had slightly grey hair, same length, same clothes, same shoes, but his complexion was much more...alive.

The paramedics quickly put the dead man on a gurney and continued to do CPR as they wheeled him into the waiting ambulance. The paramedic seemed to take it personally that the man he was working on wasn't responding. Every second he pushed his chest in and with every effort he begged the man to breathe.

"Come on! Come on!"

The twin got up and stood motionless, seemingly unable to move or even decide what to do. They put the man in the ambulance. Nobody talked to the twin standing alone and afraid. And nobody was going to.

As the crowd thinned and the man stood there, dazed and confused, I could see he was finally realizing he was dead.

He looked around and saw me staring at him. We locked eyes. He didn't care who I was or what I was or why I could see him (and nobody else seemed to be able to). He just wanted somebody, anybody, to tell him what to do. I pointed with my eyes to the ambulance and said "Go." And like a child being told something for the first time, he simply said okay and walked toward the ambulance. I never saw him again.

As the ambulance stayed parked, I noticed that bright white hue lift; all that was left were the emergency lights that eventually were shut off as the ambulance slowly drove away.

In the days that followed I thought a lot about that man. I thought how shocked he was that he was dead. I thought how scared he appeared when he finally figured it out. I thought about how he would have given anything just to be back in that heavy body once more and I thought about how sad he felt being so alone. I was also reminded how permanent death really is. When you're done, you're really done. That's it, game over. And there was such a clear boundary between the living and the dead. Seeing that once again reminded me that earthbound spirits do not belong here.

But mostly I thought about how things that we think are so important really aren't. The last thing he cared about wasn't what kind of car he drove or what iPhone he had.

What we see as a *must have* really means nothing.

That night brought a lot of clarity to me and answered my questions. Maybe I don't have all the answers, but I know they're out there. I know answers come in many forms and in many ways and that day mine was as simple as "Go to the store." For that man, it was as simple as "Just go."

Buddy

Every once in a while, a person comes into your life who impacts you in ways it takes years to understand. My friend Buddy was one of those people for me.

"Buddy," as he was nicknamed by friends, was a famous actor that I met through our mutual friend Melanie Griffith. He was going through a change in his life and was curious if things were going to get better. Usually when I talk to celebrities for the first time, they're cautious because they think I'm going to pick up things about them that I might not like. If it's a phone reading, some have gone as far as to disguise their voices or change their names so I won't guess who they are. But Buddy wasn't that kind of person. He was the guy you hoped he'd be—down to earth, blunt, and happy to chat.

That first time we talked, it was like talking to a long-lost friend. We covered everything from horses to music, and it wasn't all about him. He also seemed interested in what my life was about. He told me he had talked to a few psychics before, so the whole thing wasn't new to him, but the way he talked to me made me think he actually cared about my point of view. That never happens when I talk to celebs. They can be nice as pie but you still get the clear feeling that you're no more than a distraction or a curiosity (which is fine, because most of the time I don't exactly want to hang out with them either). But Buddy was different. I *did* want to hang out with him.

We started talking all the time. He had this zest for life and always wanted to know more about the ins and outs of what I did. I had gotten jaded through the years—people were disappointing, my job was disappointing, money was always tight. I didn't know what I was doing anymore. My dog was depressed. It all just felt hard. But when Buddy came along, that changed. As we kept talking I noticed I was relying on him more than he was relying on me. His "never say die" attitude and his fearlessness with taking chances was how I wanted to be. I actually admired the guy, and I hadn't admired anybody since JFK. I found myself needing to talk to him. He just made sense to me. He wasn't shy about calling me out for feeling sorry for myself on my dark cloud days.

I was having knee issues and was told I needed surgery. He told me about all the physical issues he had as a dancer, football player, and actor doing stunts. He told me to "grow a pair and fight through the pain." It was exactly what I needed to hear.

We talked about confidence—real confidence, not fake. And we talked about love, being willing to love unconditionally and without fear. Buddy helped me remember all the things I used to know effortlessly.

One beautiful summer day I was golfing with strangers at a fancy golf course not far from my house. As we were teeing off, my phone started to ring. I always shut it off when I golf so I thought it was odd that it was ringing. Still, I figured whoever it was would leave a message and I could get on with my game. But the phone never stopped ringing. They kept calling and calling me like a mental person. Finally, when I noticed the older gentlemen wearing knickers couldn't finish his backswing because my phone was disrupting his shot, I decided to answer the damn thing.

"Holy shit! Holy shit!" I heard several voices say, in what seemed to be the background of the call.

"Hello?" I said.

"How ya doing?" Buddy asked.

"Well, I'm golfing at the moment. Is everything okay?"

"Oh, that's nice. How's the weather?" he asked. "Anybody wearing knickers?"

Buddy always had a great sense of humor.

"Actually, yes," I said, staring at the knickers-wearing man who was now staring daggers at me due to his desire to tee off. "Can I call you back?"

"Oh yeah, sure, no problem," he said.

I heard some yelling again, followed by another "Holy shit!" in the background.

"Are you in a fight with someone?" I asked.

"I'm flying my plane, actually," he said with a laugh. "That's why I'm calling. I think I'm going to crash—well actually I'm certain I'm going to crash—and I'm wondering if it's going to be bad?"

I took a second to soak this in.

"You're actually going to crash and you're calling me to see if it's going to be bad? JESUS!" I said, tuning in to his situation. "Well, I think you'll survive just fine, but holy crap!"

"Yeah, I know I'll survive, but will I get in trouble for the beer?" he asked again, between screams in the background.

"You have beer?" I asked.

I was holding my phone standing near three uppity golfers who were anxious to get on with their game, while I counseled a famous actor about his impending plane crash.

"It actually doesn't feel like it will be too bad," I said, trying to keep my voice down. "But holy crap, Buddy!!"

"I can't believe you golf," he said. "Thanks for picking up. Call you later!"

I heard yells, and then the phone went dead.

I stood there looking at my phone until I heard Mr. Knickers guy clearing his throat. I looked up and noticed all three guys staring at me with their mouths open.

"Your shot," knickers man said.

While I had trouble focusing on the rest of my golf game, Buddy and his passengers survived the crash just fine. He seemed to be invincible—larger than life. Always seizing the day.

So, when Buddy called me one cold January day to talk about his health and his concern that there might be something wrong, I didn't worry. Even when he told me he had been diagnosed with cancer, it still felt like it was going to be okay. He told me about his new television series and he said he was doing his best work. His spirits were high and he was optimistic about what was to come. And as I hung up the phone, I couldn't help but feel optimistic myself. But a minute after I put the phone down, that changed. I remember it like you would a huge event like 9/11 or the Kennedy assassination. I took a step to go to the kitchen and I heard the words, "He's going to die, you need to accept it," in a calming soft voice. I knew that voice wasn't mine.

My father had died a few years earlier and, as I've mentioned, I see death all the time in my line of work. But this was the first time I wasn't able to comprehend the idea of another human being dying. Like with Denny later in my life, the thought of Buddy's passing was too much to imagine.

I kept what I heard to myself and tried to apply all I had been taught about death to ease my mind. *He'll be in the light. He won't be alone. There's no such thing as death. Blah, blah, blah.* But none of it seemed to matter. I didn't care that there was no such thing as death. I didn't care that his soul would be free and maybe even visit me somehow. I just didn't want my friend to die.

We talked a few times before Buddy passed, about death and how nobody escapes it. We talked about friends and the life he knew, but we kept it short because his energy was shifting.

The day Buddy died I was at the store. It was a beautiful fall day in Minnesota, and as I rounded the corner to another aisle, I felt this wave of sadness like you'd imagine they felt in *Star Wars* when a planet was destroyed. I called his wife to confirm his passing and she was kind enough to take my call. She said he died peacefully with his loved ones around him, and somehow that made me feel better. She told me they were going to make preparations for his funeral and asked if I would please come. I felt honored that she would ask and I said I would try, but inside I didn't think I could.

I struggled with his death for many years. Even losing my amazing mother, Mae, somehow seemed easier than the loss of Buddy.

And then one day I was golfing at the same hole I was at when he called me years earlier. I was lining up my shot when I swear I saw him, standing five feet in front of me, smiling and shaking his head.

"Golf," he said with a smile. "You and golf."

And then he was gone.

Buddy—and all the others who have passed and are important to us—will always be with us. I truly know that now. I may not be able to call him, but I know he's there. I can feel him. I can feel *them*.

And so can you.

The Other Side

Earlier, I said I know there's another side because I saw it. Well, I didn't exactly see the other side, but I know there's something.

When I was fifteen, life was a nightmare. I was sober, skinny, and lost. Everyone and their mother was getting high. I started too young and quit too soon.

My father was out of the house and my mother was dating a burned-out gangster.

My father was too busy hiding money, filing for bankruptcy, and moving to San Francisco to care. And my siblings were all higher than the cost of Rolling Stones tickets in 2017.

I was not a happy guy.

I thought a lot about death. What it meant to be dead, what it might feel like, how dark it was. What if everything I'd seen with my eyes or been taught until then was a lie?

Certainly my life was a lie: my friends weren't really my friends, my big shot father with his big arms and unlimited bank roll was heading for the hills, my mother was completely obsessed with a Chicago gangster she had just started dating, and my dog decided to run across the highway to commit suicide. What was real anymore?

I started to doubt everything, I didn't feel comfortable anywhere, and even sleep was difficult at best.

I didn't believe in asking God, because who's to say if somebody up there was listening?

Then one night I had a dream, the kind of dream that feels so real you can smell the grass and feel the breeze.

It started out in our basement. I was sitting on my brother's bed, pondering, when somebody came to the back door. At first I was pissed because I was comfortable. I didn't want to get up and get it, but nobody else would do it, so I went to the door.

I opened the door and there stood an angel. A full-on big wings, white cotton pants, angelic-looking guy angel. I remember thinking, "Oh fun, an angel dream. I like angel dreams."

I told him to come in, but he put out his hand and handed me a small button. It was one of those "have a nice day" buttons, the yellow smiley face kind that I hated.

I always thought it was a passive aggressive way of saying "fuck you" whenever somebody said "have a nice day." In fact, if anybody ever said that to me I'd give them the finger. Clearly I have issues.

But this was a dream, and I knew that in dreams odd things mean stuff later on, so I went with it. I thanked him and put in my pocket.

He told me his name, but for some reason that's the only part of the dream I don't remember. Everything else is still clear as a bell. He told me he wanted me to come outside, that he wanted to show me something.

He seemed like a trustworthy guy, not one of those creepy types with eyes wide open and a monotone voice, so I went with him outside. When I did, I saw this huge, beautiful, multicolored hot air balloon, just waiting for me.

The balloon itself must have been ten stories tall and seemed to fill the whole sky—dark purple, red, maroon, blue, yellow. It was something. But the baskets underneath were the amazing part; four baskets on top of each other, separated by five feet of rope, each with its own décor.

I looked at the angel and asked if I could come aboard. He said of course. He showed me where my basket was. It was the bottom basket, and for some reason it felt like home. Inside were all the things I loved: a stereo for my music, books I loved to read, pictures, and even a television. But the best part was the bed and the glass bottom floor.

I couldn't wait to take off.

The angel told me we could only go for a short time, that we had to be back soon. I was worried if I argued with him we wouldn't go at all, so I said even a short trip was better than no trip and off we went.

We slowly climbed past the trees, above the houses, and into the warm clear air just before the clouds. I felt safe, I felt at peace, and I felt as excited as I'd ever been, wondering where we might go. I couldn't wait to relax in my bed, put on some tunes, and watch the world go by.

But then we went back.

I remember telling my angel this was my dream, and that we needed to go a little longer, but he just smiled and said no.

When we landed, I didn't want to leave. I handed him back his button in the hope that it would give me more time, but he took my hand and folded it back in my palm, and he smiled.

He escorted me back to the door and told me when it was my time, he would be back. I asked him if this was for when I die, and he said it was, "but not now," and only if I finished what I was here to do.

And then I woke up. I tried so hard to fall back asleep, to look a little longer at the balloon or feel that air, but I was so excited I couldn't.

Now here's where it gets weird. When I finally gave up trying to go back to sleep, I sat up and in my hand was the button he gave me.

I've wondered for years if I fell asleep with that button in my hand or if someone put it there when I was sleeping.

But I know I didn't sleep with that button, and why would someone put that in my hand?

The only thing I know for sure is that the dream was real, and I know when I die I will see that balloon again.

GHOSTBUSTING

So, we know people die. Now what?

This chapter is about ghosts and ghostbusting. I could write a whole book just on this subject, but the purpose of this chapter is to give you a general working knowledge of how to deal with spirits or ghosts (or whatever you want to call them).

When I say ghostbusting, I mean when we or I go to a place that people claim is haunted. We identify the ghosts, if any, and we either help them cross over to the other side or we just make sure they don't stay there.

I'm going to assume that most people reading this have some understanding of the possibility that there are ghosts. Unless you've lived under a rock the last fifty years, I don't see how you couldn't believe at least a little.

With all the videos, the sound recordings, the eyewitnesses, and the testimonials of non-psychic people, you'd really have to have one closed-minded dolt to not at least entertain the fact that there might be ghosts.

Don't get me wrong, I love denial. I've got a place on the River Denial myself, but come on! Really? You still think thirty-five million people are just making this stuff up?

I'm also going to also assume you're not a complete idiot. If you have an open mind, even if it's a razor-thin open mind, I can work with you.

Let's start with the basics.

It is my belief that when you die, your soul leaves your body. I've actually seen souls leave their bodies when a person dies, which is why I believe that.

Now in most cases, that soul goes to the other side. Some say heaven, some say hell, you never hear Cleveland, but who's to say.

As I explained in the last chapter, I know that most go someplace. People with more depth than me seem to know the answer to that, I'm just going with what I know.

But some don't go anywhere. They stay earthbound and they do so for a variety of reasons. Some are afraid to go to wherever, some feel guilt, some feel compelled to stay for unfinished business—a murder, an accidental suicide, a loved one they can't leave behind. Something prevents them from crossing over to the light.

So these souls are just here, floating around, confused, angry, sad, generally not in the best place. I don't think I've ever run across an earthbound spirit that was happy as hell to be hanging around. Not saying it's not possible, just saying I've never come across one. But I've come across plenty who were pissed that they were dead.

And these souls don't have a lot of people to talk to, there's not a lot to do. They have the occasional psychic they can bug, but psychics are about as fun as sitting in the teachers' lounge. They're harder to scare. So they hang around houses that are familiar, families they might know, places they liked to hang out in—bars, theatres, parks. Any places where the living like to hang out.

You want to know where ghosts *don't* hang out? Cemeteries! Cemeteries are one of the quietest places on earth to be, as far as ghostly activity. The old-time psychics used to picnic in cemeteries because they were so peaceful. Sure, the occasional ghost will stop by to see their headstone or watch a visitor, but after that it's Sizzler, here we come.

The problem is that when these ghosts get bored, when they want attention, or when you do construction at your house or business, they get bugged. They get bugged by change, by boredom, and by limitations, so they move things, play with the lights, scare the pets, create smells, anything to get a rise from the people around them or show their discontent.

Following me so far?

Most people who have never experienced a ghost encounter freak out when they notice something like that. They build it up to be demonic or evil. They assume from the movies they've seen or the stories they've heard that these ghosts are going to enter their bodies, turn them into zombies, eat their kid's brains, and make them write bad checks. This fear only makes things worse, because now the ghosts are getting what they want.

This is where I come in.

People call me or other busters and tell us their story. In my case, I refer most of the calls I get to people who actually care. That sounds terrible, I know, but unless the walls are bleeding or your cat's floating above your kitchen table, I get a little bored. And the last thing these people need is a bored ghostbuster.

They're scared, alone, and embarrassed. When they call, most of them will apologize for having these issues. It's almost like they feel unclean or soiled because of what's happening. And most think they're going crazy.

Why am I not more sympathetic if I know these people are hurting? Because I'm a dick.

Ninety percent of the calls I get are simple, run-of-the-mill ghostbusting jobs. You go in, identify the ghost, talk to it, find out why it's there, and send it on its way. When I say send it on its way, I mean into the light. There's always a light or an exit they can take if they want to, and most of the time they do.

It becomes a counseling session more than anything. Why haven't they left? Are they angry? What are they angry about? Are they scared? What happened to frighten them? Does somebody in the house bother them? What do they do to bother them? On and on.

A majority of these conversations take place in the dark, in the attic, in the basement, or in some weird crawl space.

From the outsider it probably looks strange, but from my point of view it's pretty boring stuff.

They do try to test you, blow in your face, make noises, pull your hair. But once you establish that you're there to get them to leave and not to play games, the drama dies down and you can do your thing.

Keep in mind, ghosts have no right to be here. They're dead. Their lives are over; like it or not, they need to move on. It doesn't matter if they don't like the new wall or the new boyfriend. They have to go. They have no power over you. In fact it's just the opposite. You have all the power. If more people knew this, they wouldn't need ghostbusters; they would simply take care of it themselves. And they can! I don't have special powers! I've just done it a million times.

Imagine you have some weird guy walk in your house and stand there. Maybe he turns the light on and off or moves the remote when you're watching TV. What if he blew in your ear right at the good part of the show? You wouldn't jump up on the furniture and scream, or grab a cross and wave it around. And I'm pretty sure you wouldn't

run out of the house with your arms above your head, screaming "AUNTIE EM! AUNTIE EM!" No, you'd kick him out.

Take the fear out, and remember that they have no
right to be there. Talk to the ghost if you want, but don't
put up with their crap. You didn't die! They did. Demand
that they leave.

The tough ones are when the people who are living get
too close to the ghost that's haunting them. They try to
make friends, make them their pet, or worse, get emotion-
ally and physically involved with the spirit. When that happens, it's a whole different deal. Now you need *their* help in
getting rid of the spirit.

When I teach ghostbusting classes, I put my students
in the scariest room of the scariest haunted house I can find
and have then perform a séance. You would never do that
in an actual ghostbusting job, because it's stupid. It's like a
Ouija board on steroids.

But for ghostbusting school it helps the students face
their fears and empowers them. After a night or two of that,
they can go anywhere.

That's what you want: an empowered ghostbuster, not
some dipstick puffing out his chest, screaming "Show yourself! I'm not afraid of you!!"

That's embarrassing.

The number one rule in ghostbusting is to always walk
in with protection. As I've said before, protection is picturing yourself surrounded by white light.

The reason why this is important is twofold. First, when you walk into a house that feels heavy, dark, and negative, if you feel the light around you, it changes the mood of the house. It gives the sense that you're there to get the job done, not to stir things up.

Second, the spirits can't get to you. You're protected. This means less activity and less chance of things getting out of hand.

Another important part of dealing with a ghost is being unafraid. You're always going to be a little nervous; some people get nervous watching *SpongeBob SquarePants*. But I'm talking about confidence in what you're doing and your ability to handle it.

I've been on a few jobs where a priest or shaman has run out because it tested their faith. Spirits will do that, especially dark ones. They will go to the place you feel the most vulnerable and try to exploit it. You don't let that happen; you walk in knowing you belong there and they don't.

The first fifty ghostbustings can be spooky: the people are scared, they tell spooky stories, if you've got some guy playing the organ in the background, it makes you nervous.

The next fifty, it becomes routine. You stop being nervous and you concentrate more on the task at hand.

For me there are three parts to a ghostbusting.

The first part is the story. You go in, sit down, and the person who called or is affected by it tells you the story—when it began, what happens, when it happens, who is affected.

The story is important because finally the people involved have someone who will listen to them and not freak out. It also helps to gauge how many and how strong the entities are. If the lights are just going on and off, or you feel a chill in a room or two, you know your night won't be that tough. If pets are being thrown around and walls are oozing dark red liquids, you know it's going to be a long night.

Once you hear the story, you move on to phase two: the exploration phase.

In this phase, you go through the house and see for yourself, what, if any, ghosts, cold spots, or places with creepy vibes there are. You also find out which room is ground zero, the place with the most activity.

After phase two, you meet in a neutral spot—somewhere there hasn't been any real activity—and come up with a game plan. You discuss what you saw, what you felt, your concerns, your questions. You come up with where you want to start and a rough plan for what you're going to do.

You tell the host your plans, find out if they have any objections, and move on to phase three, the actual busting.

Can you start to see how after one hundred of these jobs you might get bored?

In phase three, you always start at the worst place in the house, the place where most of the negative energy is. You do this for a couple of reasons. In the beginning, your energy is stronger. You're fresher.

Some ghosts have the ability to take energy from you. They tap into your light and suck it out to make themselves stronger. If you put protection around yourself, that's less likely to happen. Again, when I say protection, I mean visualizing a white light around you—God's light. Still, the longer you're at the job, the more tired you become. So always start at the strongest point.

The second reason you start there is because if you go right to the place where the entities hang out, they know you're not afraid of them. That's important. You want to establish that you're not there to play games or show how tough you are. Your job is to get rid of whatever is there so the living people can relax.

Ghostbusting isn't glamorous. It's a lot of long, tedious conversations with people, living and dead, and at the end of the night, there's no guarantee that all your time spent had any effect.

That's why, on most ghostbusting jobs, the beginning part is always the best part. There's a little drama, a little anticipation. Things are more apt to happen in the beginning, when the spirits are testing your resolve.

Instead of telling you spooky ghost stories, I want to show you examples of situations that come up when you do a job.

I've taught classes with a lot of people in them and I've taught classes with smaller groups.

In each class, I try to bring the people to actual ghost-bustings. Have them experience what it's like to actually deal with a ghost.

Two of my favorite people to work with were my friends Therese and Paul.

I first met Therese several years ago when she called me about a possible ghost at her son's house in St. Paul. It sounded like a pretty simple job, bumps in the night, shadows here and there. But another student needed experience, so I agreed and went, along with my student. I met Therese and her husband at their son's house.

Right when I pulled up I saw a female spirit looking at me from the bedroom window. She looked more nervous than angry, so I knew the job would be fast.

Introductions were made and we went through the house. My student, Bob, talked to Therese and her husband while I took care of the spirit.

As I suspected, she wasn't there to haunt anybody, she was just lost. Ian, Therese's son, has that light that spirits love. A lot of folks have it, but don't know it or know what to do with it.

The job itself took about ten minutes, but it's always the questions from the living that take the most time.

I liked Therese right off the bat. She was about 5'2" with the energy of a hummingbird on crack. Her husband was the more laid-back of the two, and not really a believer. Still, they were both happy we came and the problem was fixed.

A couple of months later I got another call from Therese, following up on the job we did. It turned out that she and her husband lived about a mile down the road from me. I didn't take payment for the job and she felt bad. She offered me Twins tickets and said that if I was interested, she'd leave them on her door.

That was the extent of our relationship for a couple of years. She'd call when she had extra tickets and leave them outside her door, until one day she asked if I could give her a reading.

We did the reading. During it, we talked about a lot of things, one of them being her interest in psychics and ghostbusting.

I told her if one came up she could come along. Sure enough, shortly after we talked, one did.

I got a call from a lady who lived about forty-five minutes from where I lived.

She said there had been a lot of activity at her house and it was hard for her to be there when her husband was away.

The thought of driving all the way out there so this lady could sleep didn't exactly pull my toffee. In fact, I think at first I turned her down. But several calls later her urgency seemed to be getting stronger, and I agreed to come out.

I asked Therese if she'd like to come along, and she was into it.

By the time we got there, I was pissed. It was waaay out there and I knew this job was going to be stupid. I pulled into the driveway and as I did, a monster black truck pulled in behind me.

I gathered my ghostbusting stuff and started to walk toward the house. From behind me, I heard an angry man asking me who the fuck I was. I turned around, and there walking toward me was this muscle-bound bald guy, clearly upset, and wearing a gun.

I returned his question with a question of my own, "Who the fuck are you?" I asked. I really didn't know who he was or why he was so pissed.

But that made him even more pissed. "I live here, pretty boy. Why are you here?" he asked. This guy looked nuts, and he didn't seem like the kind of guy you fucked around with. His eyes were dark and intense. He looked right at me, like he was figuring out where he was going to hit me first.

I thought it best I ease up on being a dick and go with the truth.

"Your wife called me. She said you've got a ghost problem, that's why we are here," I told him. Now his attention went to his wife, Shirley.

"God damn it, Shirley, why is this fucking pretty boy in my driveway?" he said as he brushed by me. I looked at Therese, but she seemed just as dumbfounded as I was. "Wait here," she said, and proceeded to go toward the house. I followed.

I could hear the man and his wife arguing over why I was there. She agreed that she did call me, but insisted I needed to be there. Her husband (Paul) didn't want me anywhere near the property, let alone near him. I think his exact words were, "Keep that fucker away from me."

If the place hadn't been so far away, I would have said "screw this" and left. But no way was I going to drive all the way back after driving all that way to get there. Besides, if my being there was going to piss this guy off even more, I'd stay all night.

Shirley met us at the entry. She looked embarrassed. "Please don't worry about my husband, Paul. I don't know what he's so upset about, but it might be best if you stayed away from him."

Introductions were made and the tensions died down. I assured her I would stay away from her husband.

We went to the kitchen area and a group of women were gathered around the kitchen table. "Oh," she said, "I was going to ask if you mind giving a few readings."

Normally this would bug me. I don't like to mix the two things together. It's like dancing on a newly waxed floor. If I'm ghostbusting I like to let things settle for a bit. If I do readings before I get rid of the ghost, the ghost likes to throw their two cents in and it gets confusing.

And after a ghostbusting, I'm just too tired.

But the thought occurred to me that I could kill a couple of birds with one stone—maybe even three birds.

I could have Therese get the story with Paul. Therese got along with everybody. He wouldn't yell at her and she could find out why he hated me so much.

I could also make little money. I wasn't planning on charging these guys, even though it was on the other side of the world. When Shirley called, she said she'd had other ghostbusters out there, but they didn't do the job. She said they all charged her.

She wanted to know how much I charged.

I couldn't take her money under those circumstances. The assholes who charged her and didn't take care of the job should've given her the money back. I couldn't take her dough for the ghostbustings.

But I could charge for readings, maybe even enough to take a flight back.

I told Therese the plan and she agreed to talk to Paul. I put on my psychic cap and we started our night.

I started doing readings. One by one, the people wanting readings piled into a little den off of the kitchen. It was hard to work with all the ghosts in the house, especially because they kept asking me to talk to Paul. But I valued my life. I wasn't going near Paul.

In between readings, Therese would come in and give me updates on Paul.

"Boy, he sure doesn't like you," was her first report, and with each following report it only got worse. By the third reading, she told me he wanted to kill me.

Now it was almost impossible to concentrate on the readings because the ghosts were insistent that I talk to Paul, and Therese was ready to call in SWAT.

By this time, Paul was sitting in the living room watching the Wild play hockey. They were losing, which wasn't helping his mood.

I decided to confront the situation. I've always been a huge fan of sticking my hand in the meat grinder, and there was a big one in the living room.

I walked up behind him. Without turning around, he told me to get the fuck away from him. I asked him, "Why do you suppose you're having such a negative reaction to me? We don't even know each other."

I asked him to come and talk to me.

He said no.

Then I put my hands on his bald, mean head. "What the fuck are you doing?" he asked, and then he began to sweat like he was taking a shower.

"Just come on and talk to me," I said, "just for a second."

I think he was so confused by the sweat that he figured fuck it, why not.

We went into the room where I was doing readings and we began to talk. At first, he repeated his disdain for me. Therese asked him why and he couldn't think of an answer. "I just do," he said, so I moved on.

I asked him why all these ghosts wanted me to talk to him. He didn't know that either. I tried the hand to his head thing again, and again he started to sweat.

The hand to the head thing is a grounding technique Birdie had taught me years before. When a person feels "gone" or "drifting" you're supposed to grab the person's hand or head.

Paul's mitts were too close to his massive arms to try to attempt that, so the shiny dome seemed the best option.

He seemed shocked at the sweat that was pouring from his head. I was a little surprised myself, and Therese was downright owl-eyed.

But the more he sweat, the less angry he became and the more talkative he was.

Turns out Paul was a cop. The ghosts in the house were all about him. They wanted him to use his psychic abilities. He had experiences when he was a kid, but now, at this time in his life, they needed him to see it and use it.

We went through the house. All the activity was coming from Paul's bedroom or spare room, where he would sleep when he got in late.

He also showed me where a couple of idiot ghost-busters came in and drew Celtic symbols on the wall with this permanent, invisible marker, as a way of warding off ghosts. No wonder he hated me; he probably thought I was going to charge him four hundred bucks to chant.

By the end of the night, we had become friends. We agreed to talk again, and a week later we contacted each other. He wanted to know more; the door was open and he was ready to walk through.

So was Therese. Maybe not as much as Paul, but she was very curious about it all. And besides, those two got along like peas and carrots.

I agreed to teach them both the ins and outs of the ghostbusting world, and off we went.

When it came to rule number one, Paul and Therese both got a D-minus in that part of class.

Paul's attitude was more "Fuck it, I'm going in," while Therese's attitude was "Crap, I left the iron on."

They both had psychic abilities, but they both struggled with how to deal with them.

Therese would get feelings about people she knew and places she'd been to. She also was really good with business ideas, knowing the things that were going to be big in a year or two. Problem was that she doubted herself. Even though she could see the ideas she had a year ago were now the next big thing, she didn't trust herself enough to act on them when she first had the feeling. Like she said, she would have been a millionaire if she had just trusted herself on one of the ideas that she got.

Therese has a son who bought a house not far from my house. The plan was to completely gut the house and modernize it to resell.

One night when Therese was at the house alone, she felt a presence before she even went in. She called me and asked me if I'd come over. I said I would, and within five minutes I was there.

Therese had a worried look on her face. This wasn't alarming, Therese was known to be a bit jumpy. In fact, that was one of the reasons I liked her. If there was the slightest activity, Therese would feel it immediately. Basically my human version of a canary in a coal mine.

The house itself was under construction—torn out walls, exposed wiring and staircases, ripped up flooring, a complete remodel. There was no electricity, so we had to be careful where we walked. We used our phones to light the way.

As we walked in the house, I could tell right away that the place was active. A whirlwind of activity was blowing through the house, as if a mini tornado was in the room.

A man directly in front of me was giving me the stink eye, and I could smell the whiskey on his breath. He didn't want us there. As I looked around further, I saw a woman in the corner and a little girl with a cat in the living room. The air was thick, heavy. It was hard to breathe.

I looked over at Therese. She was visibly uncomfortable. She asked how a cat got into the house. I reminded her that it wasn't alive. It was time to leave.

I was surprised by how bad this place was. I didn't want to alarm Therese, but those spirits were angry. If I had to actually bust this house, it would take all night.

As we left, she confessed to feeling ill. I asked her if she had put protection around herself and she looked dumbfounded.

Prior to me going to the house, Paul and Therese had come to my house every week to discuss ghostbusting. And every week we discussed putting protection over yourself.

If you go in unprotected, it's very common to feel queasy when there are a lot of spirits around, especially if they have ill will toward you.

The good news was that this was a perfect place to teach Therese and Paul.

My experience teaching them brought up some good advice that might be beneficial to other new ghostbusters.

#1: Always Have a Buddy When You Ghostbust!

A couple days later, all three of us went back to the house. Again, when we walked into the house, it was full of activity. I asked Therese (whose nickname from Paul was Minnie) if she'd protected herself, and she said she had. But with Therese, you never really knew. She could have forgotten and just didn't want me to yell at her, so she probably did it right after I asked.

Paul, on the other hand, was more of a commando kind of guy. When I asked him if he put protection around himself, he shouted, "Fuck that, let's go."

So we went in.

Another drawback to not protecting yourself is that it attracts other spirits to come in. Just like turning on the porch light brings in bugs. But for the purposes of teaching,

I let it go. Besides, Paul was the kind of guy you had to show things, not tell.

In the two days since I was there, there was clearly more construction going on. And there was also more activity.

The place felt darker, like the party was getting bigger.

Now there were open walls and scaffolding. They managed to have one light in the house, but otherwise it was completely dark.

Whiskey-a-go-go, the drunk, angry guy I saw when I first went in with Therese, was waiting for us at the door, still angry.

The feeling in the house was like we were intruding. A strong pressure was in the air. I decided to be more of a tour guide rather than a ghostbuster. I wanted Therese and Paul to be exposed to as much as they could handle. I wanted them to trust what they saw and felt. This wasn't a normal, run-of-the-mill haunted house. This place was bad.

Therese was our ghost detector. Every time she would see someone or something, she would gasp. Naturally we would both turn our attention to what she saw, but this can be a tad unnerving, in the dark, in a haunted house, with nails sticking up everywhere.

But again, for the purposes of what I wanted them to learn, it was good.

Paul had a harder time with her gasping. Every time she'd yelp, Paul would yell, "Jesus Christ, Minnie, stop gasping!"

We decided to tackle the upstairs first. There was a heavy, angry feeling coming from the upstairs bedroom, and we always start at the place that feels the worst.

The house itself had a dangerous feel to it. You never knew if you were going to trip on something or fall through something. Add the element of all the activity, ghost-wise, and it had you on edge.

We made our way up the exposed winding stairway, using our phones for light. We probably should have brought flashlights, but I never liked that visual. A flashlight has a more direct beam. You shine your light around a room and then all of a sudden you see this pale, dark-eyed dead girl standing there, staring at you. Reminded me of when I was young.

We got to the bedroom and sure enough, it was bad.

In the beginning, Therese didn't truly trust herself. Instead of saying "There's a ghost," she would ask, "Is that a ghost?" One or both of us would confirm it or deny if we didn't see one. But when Therese kept asking, "Is that a ghost, is that a ghost?" we couldn't keep up with how many were in the room.

There were spirits in the bedroom, spirits in the bathroom. Paul was being hit by nails and debris. We could hear people talking, whispering.

Therese must have protected herself, because so far she wasn't sick. Paul, on the other hand, was getting dizzy.

I decided to take them out of the upstairs and bring them to the basement. It was getting to be too much upstairs, and I was stuck. I didn't want to get rid of any of the ghosts that were around, but I think they sensed that, because things were really heating up.

I thought the basement might be a little break from the heaviness upstairs.

Basements are generally creepy. People don't always live in the basement, and because there isn't a life force energy there, the dead feel bigger.

Still, it felt like it would be a normal creepy, not this "you're going to die any second" creepy we were all feeling.

As I was walking toward the top of the stairs, I made a sarcastic remark about coming back to deal with the assholes in the bedroom. Then I felt a push on my back. Not a strong one, like I have in the past, but just enough to throw me off balance. And with no hand railings, I could have fallen. But Paul grabbed my waist and stopped me. It happened so quick; if he didn't have such fast reflexes, I would have broken my neck. That's why you always need a buddy.

#2: Avoid Wearing Buttoned Shirts or Zippers

After thanking Paul, we made our way downstairs to the basement.

When we got there, it was a different vibe—more rambunctious, mischievous. It didn't feel evil, like the one upstairs did.

Still, it was unnerving.

The basement was set up like a big rectangle. As you came down the stairs, across the room was a utility room with a washer and dryer. To the left was a big window. The room was filled with all the tools the construction workers were using. This made walking freely difficult.

There was someone close to the utility room. Therese noticed it first. It was a dark cloud-looking thing with no face or movement. When she asked if that was a ghost, Paul told her to shut up. Then Therese told him to shut up and then they were fighting.

Those two fought a lot. Paul would usually start it, but Therese was more than happy to join in. It would stop when Paul would threaten to kill Therese and then Therese would punch Paul.

Those two didn't care where they were, they would still fight. Therese would say something Paul thought was stupid or Paul would make a remark and Therese would punch him. I just rolled my eyes most of the time and hoped neither one killed the other. Therese stabbed Paul once at a restaurant with a fork, but that's another story.

While those two were going at it, I went to the part of the basement where the window was. I tried to see if the mist looked different from a different angle. I asked if one of them would go to the spot where the mist seemed strongest, and of course they both fought for who would go. They both went.

When they got to where it seemed darkest, Paul flashed his phone around and yelled at Therese. "Jesus Christ, Minnie, your shirt's unbuttoned!" Sure enough, she looked down and her button-down shirt was fully unbuttoned.

She grabbed her shirt and called Paul a perv. "I didn't touch you," he said, "Don't you think you would have noticed if I did?" The now embarrassed Therese buttoned her shirt. "Well I didn't do it," she said, "One of you clowns must have." I reminded her that I was on the other side of the room, but that didn't ease her comfort level.

Paul, who by this time had made his way to the bottom of the stairs, yelled out, "Does it seem a little chilly in here to you two?" I flashed my phone in his direction. Paul had pulled his pants down to his ankles.

"What the hell's going on here?" he said.

Levity may sound disrespectful in cases like this, but it actually helps. In many ghost jobs, it's a very heavy environment. If you can lighten the mood, you can deal with the spirits easier. That night it was needed.

#3: Electronics Will Do Odd Things, It's Just a Part of What Happens

Paul pulled up his pants and walked back to where we were both standing.

I told them both they needed to concentrate, but neither one of them were in the mood. They continued to fight— Therese said it wasn't funny and that she didn't unbutton her shirt, Paul accused her of being a stripper.

I walked toward the part of the room with the most construction equipment, and as I did, my phone lit up, then played the creepiest version of the Humpty Dumpty song I'd ever heard.

Therese and Paul shut up. "What the fuck was that?" Paul asked. "I don't know," I replied and continued to look at my phone.

"Let me see that thing," Paul said as he walked toward me. Again my phone started playing Humpty Dumpty. I didn't have Humpty Dumpty on my playlist, *anywhere*. Paul started getting creeped out. "Seriously dude, stop playing that fucking song."

I told him I was a grown man—why would I have that on my phone? But he was convinced that I was somehow playing it. He examined my phone and couldn't figure out what was going on. Then it happened again.

Now he was really creeped out. "Holy fuck, what is with your phone?" he asked, and then told us both that he was going upstairs.

My phone didn't play that song again, ever. And how they made that happen still puzzles me.

But it did get our attention, and maybe that was the point.

It's not unusual for lights to go on and off or clocks to stop. I've been on jobs where the stove will turn on and the doorbells will ring. It's all a part of what happens when you deal with this stuff. Still, that was creepy.

We went upstairs and the house was very much alive. Paul was pretty dizzy by this time, and we decided we would come back in another few days.

We continued to go back to that house, and each time we did, there was new activity. Apparently the workers liked to smoke dope when they worked, which not only pissed the current ghosts off, but brought in new ones to party.

If this was an actual busting, we wouldn't have let it get so bad. But this was more of a training exercise than a professional ghostbusting. I wanted things to get bad so Therese and Paul could be exposed to it.

Eventually we did clear the house, but it took a long time.

It takes a while for that feeling to leave you, once you go through something like that. But they both faced fears they had about being in a situation like that, and I have to say, they did really well.

Paul and Therese would go on a lot of jobs with me and they always turned out really fun, no matter how badly haunted the place was.

And because we had so much fun, it made the jobs really easy and lightened the places up, wherever we went.

The Bad Side of Ghostbusting Jobs

A job that wasn't so fun was one I did with my sister Echo. We did this job not far from the city we both lived in.

We got a call from a landlord who said her tenant, a young man in his early thirties, was acting strangely. She said she had gone to the apartment a couple of times, and when she did, he only met her outside the apartment first. He asked that she not mention any females while in the apartment and not be too friendly to him while she was there. She assumed he had a girl with him, but whenever she went in, he was alone. She said she called us because she could feel the presence of someone in the apartment. She said she asked him if he ever noticed anything and he immediately said no and asked her to leave.

Prior to this, I wasn't a big believer in ghosts being intimate with the living. I had heard about it, but I just had a hard time believing it. It seemed like something somebody would say to get attention or to be odd, which wasn't that uncommon in my world.

When we arrived, we were met outside by the landlord, a woman in her sixties named Nancy. She told us she had a talk with her tenant, Derrick, about us coming over, and at first he was opposed to the idea. But her concern for his mental health, along with her property, convinced him to at least let us come in and meet him.

Normally, people are relieved to see us, finally feeling like someone might understand the goings on that they've had to deal with. But knowing Derrick wasn't exactly happy we were coming made this job feel odd right off the bat.

Derrick met us at the door. I was surprised by how tall he was, about 6'5", maybe 240 pounds, with sandy blonde hair and glasses. My first impression was how shy he seemed; he didn't make eye contact and preferred looking at the floor rather than at us. He didn't engage in conversation, just a simple "Hello, how do you do" when introductions were made. But he didn't come across as rude, just shy.

We all sat down, Echo, Nancy, and myself on one side of the room, Derrick facing us on the other. An awkward silence filled the room until Nancy broke it by explaining to Derrick why she asked us to come to his house. She went over the conversation the two had earlier about what she was concerned with, and what we did, and asked him again if everything was okay.

I, like Derick, wasn't sure what the hell we were doing there. Was there an actual ghost or was this guy just off his nut? I could feel someone in the room, but they weren't making their presence known and I wasn't in the mood to play find the spook.

After Nancy's question to Derrick, he became visibly anxious. He stood up and started walking around, pacing. Echo stepped in and asked if he was okay. He looked stressed. He said, "She's here and she doesn't like you two being here."

Echo and I looked at each other like wtf.

I asked him to please sit down and explain what was going on, but instead he walked into the kitchen and started having a conversation with himself. Now I started to think he was crazy. I rolled my eyes at Echo and got up and went into the kitchen. He was a big guy, so I didn't want to upset him, but my patience with ghost drama had worn off by '75. He seemed surprised that I followed him to the kitchen. I again asked him to please come sit and explain what was going on, and this time he did.

He sat down, and with his head down, in a calm, quiet voice said, "Linda doesn't like you guys being here."

"Linda?" Echo asked, and again Derrick became quiet.

By now it was getting stupid. I didn't know if this guy was a mental case or just needing attention. Judging by the sparse way his house was set up—very little furniture, no TV, a lonely plant here and there—it didn't look like he did much socializing. Maybe he was just one of the people who did this for attention or company.

I said, "Look Derrick, I don't know what's going on, but if you don't want us here, we can leave."

He stood up again and said, "Okay fine, I'll show you, but she's going to be mad, I'm just warning you." And with that he walked back into the kitchen.

I looked at Echo like "Seriously?" and got up and walked toward the kitchen with him. The kitchen was set up in an L shape. An open-door entrance with a stove and refrigerator to your left as you walked in, and if you continued straight you'd run into the kitchen sink and counter. As you turned right, a kitchen table fit snugly in the small other half, followed by another open door. When Derrick walked in, he did so at the stove and refrigerator entrance. He stopped with his back roughly against the refrigerator.

I stood outside the kitchen this time because I honestly didn't know if the guy was stable and I didn't want to hang out in such cramped quarters with a mental guy.

Now Derrick started to talk out loud to himself, pacing back and forth as he did.

"I'm bringing a girl home tonight," he said, "and you have to leave us alone." He paused, looking at the air. "She's really pretty," he continued, "and I think I like her."

I again looked over at Echo and made the "he's nuts" sign with my fingers.

Suddenly, he started to panic. "SHE'S HERE!, SHE'S HERE!" he yelled and looked at both of us with sheer terror.

Now it had that performance artist feel to it. I either needed a box of popcorn or it was time to leave.

Up to this point Echo and I hadn't seen anyone. We *felt* somebody, but we hadn't seen them. But the way this guy was acting, whatever it was was with him in the kitchen. I could see in the kitchen and I saw nothing.

Just when I was about to say "This is stupid, we're going to go," Derrick started yelling again, "I'm sorry, I'm sorry." He threw himself against the refrigerator door and turned his head back and forth violently like he was being slapped. "STOP!" he screamed, and then grabbed his chest as though he was just stabbed.

This was getting embarrassing. His performance, although semi-convincing, was just that—a performance.

I looked over at Echo to see if she agreed that we should leave, but Echo looked like she was in shock. She motioned for me to look at Derrick. I rolled my eyes and did what she asked. When I looked closer I saw Derrick's feet barely touching the ground. He was on his tippy-toes, struggling to stand. On his face, slap marks were starting to appear. I looked back at Echo and mouthed the words "holy shit," then I started to walk closer to where Derrick was standing. Just when I got to him, whatever was holding Derrick up released him. He grabbed his chest and tried to catch his breath. His buttoned plaid shirt was now unbuttoned. He looked disheveled and in pain. I asked if he was okay. In his soft voice, he said it hurt. I asked what hurt and he moved his hands to expose clear scratch marks down his chest. "My chest," he said.

"Jesus, Derrick," I said. "What the fuck was that?" I helped Derrick to the couch and told him to sit. He had the look of someone who had been through this before, embarrassed, in pain, but almost apologetic. "I told you, *her*," he said.

"Okay, Derrick," Echo said, "Start from the beginning."

Derrick went on to explain that when he moved into the house, he was lonely. He said he wasn't from around here and only came to get a decent job, but all he did was work all the time, come home, then go back to work. He said he didn't have any friends here and his weekends were spent just watching TV and sleeping.

He said that about a year ago, this spirit showed up, a woman. He described her as being in her mid-thirties, attractive, with shoulder-length, sandy blonde hair. He said she called herself Linda.

At first it scared him. He didn't know what to think or if he should tell somebody. He was certain that if he did, they would think he was crazy, so he kept it to himself. But, he said, she was nice to him. She was friendly, always happy to see him. She didn't do weird things like play with the stereo and lights. She would greet him when he got home, and after a while, he said he looked forward to coming home and talking with her. He did wonder at some point if he had lost his marbles, but she felt so real, and he liked her company.

He said she complimented him about his appearance, suggested he start working out so he would like himself more, and generally seemed to care whether he was happy or not.

Then Derrick stopped talking.

All three of us looked at each other, mesmerized by what he had to say so far and wanting to hear more. But Derrick wasn't talking, he just stared at the ground and shuffled his feet.

Finally, I asked him if he was alright. He lifted his head slightly and with that small voice said, "We became intimate."

A sinking feeling came over me. I had heard of women being intimate with male spirits and somehow mechanically that made sense, but when Derrick said that he had been intimate, I had a hard time picturing it. I wasn't going to assume he was nuts—something left those marks on his chest—but...really?

I asked him what he meant by intimate and he went on to describe how she came to him one night—he thought in a dream—and they made love. "But," he said, "it wasn't a dream."

I was taught a long time ago not to judge. We all are a tad off and I didn't want to call him a liar because, like I said, the marks were real, so I asked him to continue, even though I was having a hard time wrapping my brain around this one.

He said this continued for months, each time getting better and better. He couldn't wait to go to bed.

At this point we were all crossing our legs and squirming in our seats. The tension was a bit thick, so to break that tension, I said with a smile, "Talk about safe sex," but Echo gave me the stink eye, so I went back to shutting up.

He said everything was fine, he was feeling more confident, stronger about himself, so much so that he thought maybe he could date a real person. And he said when he told Linda that he was thinking about that was when the abuse started.

Now our night had gotten very complicated.

In a situation like this, you can't just get rid of the spirit. Now it's personal. The spirit has an entitlement; it couldn't care less what we say or do. You have to get the living person the spirit is involved with to do most of the heavy lifting.

They first have to really want the spirit to go, and then it's like a break-up. They have to tell the spirit it's time to leave, and we just become facilitators at that point.

We told Derrick what was needed for this to change. We spent the next three hours explaining the pros and cons of having a spirit lover, his responsibility to get rid of her, and what must change in his personal life so she wouldn't come back if he was lonely again.

On this particular job it all went smoothly. We were able to convince Derrick to let go of Linda, to get out and date someone with skin. We were able to cross Linda over to the other side, and as far as I know, the problems ended there.

You have to change the dynamic. After you've heard the spooky story and you've walked through the spooky house with the spooky noises and the spooky lights going on and off and you've seen the spooky spook, you clear yourself of all that spookiness and concentrate on just the opposite. What do you love most in this world? Think of that. What is your favorite time, favorite place? You surround yourself with those feelings. You change the dynamic from spooky to nice. Now you're ready to deal with the ghost objectively.

People ask me what the scariest ghostbusting job I ever did was. The scariest for me was when I knew the least about ghosts and ghostbusting. The more you know, the less afraid you become, because you know your strengths and you know theirs. You know they can't harm you unless you let them. You know you have the power, not them. And you know you're protected, and that alleviates most, if not all, of your fears.

PLANET HOLLYWOOD

Another thing people always ask me about is Hollywood. Do I read celebrities, how many do I do, what's so-and-so really like? They seem to think if a psychic does readings for famous actors that somehow makes them more of a legitimate psychic.

For one thing, as a psychic you aren't supposed to tell a client what you've told other clients. If you do, what's to stop them from thinking that you'll tell somebody else what you told *them* in a reading?

And if you do tell them about so-and-so, that client won't trust you enough to call you back. You'd basically be cutting your own throat for the sake of gossip.

And really, celebs aren't the high-water mark for psychics. Making a difference in a person's life, giving them hope, sparking their energy. That's the high-water mark.

It is my experience that there is a dark energy and a light energy. The dark side's job is to stop us, put self-doubt in our minds, put up blocks that make us second guess. It's not personal, it's the job of the dark side.

The light side is the faith and trust side, the belief side. If you really want something, if you really believe you deserve what you want, you'll get it.

So many normal people are stopped by the dark side. They have a dream, they try to pursue it, they hit a snag, they quit. Maybe they try a few times, and if nothing works they just give up and go back to something safe and practical. I see this every day, all day. It's disheartening, because I know they gave in to the dark side. I know if they just would have kept going they would have achieved their dreams. But they let people or circumstance stop them.

Actors who have made it and producers and writers who are successful don't listen to the dark side. Most of them are so narcissistic that they *have* to go forward. So, when I see an opportunity coming for them, I *know* they are going to take it. That's not the case with normal people. Normal people will quit.

And the ironic thing is that the dark side only stops the people who are here to make a difference. It doesn't care about you if you're not going to affect people with your success. It only seems to try to stop the people who are going to inspire other people.

The bigger the dream, the more the darkness tries to stop you. Because the dark side knows if you succeed like you're supposed to, your success will inspire others, and that's the whole point of the darkness—to stop that.

For me, that was the draw to working with people in the business.

I got started when I was a hotshot psychic in Minneapolis. I hung out at the hip places downtown and would set up readings in these places to mingle with the up-and-comers. I liked the vibe in these places, because it felt like hope. Like things were possible. And for a future psychic, that vibe is important. You want to be optimistic about life, otherwise you sound old and crotchety.

I myself wasn't a hip guy. I didn't have a nice car, I took the bus a lot (psychics don't make much dough), I always spilled my coffee or tripped over a chair. But just being around those places made people think better of me, and I really did like the vibes.

One day I was at a place called the New French Café. It wasn't new, and it didn't look much like a café, but a lot of the artists, local actors, producers, and the occasional hairdresser hung out there. It was located in what they used to call the Warehouse District, but is now called the North Loop.

I was doing a reading for an up-and-coming producer named Jon. Everybody liked Jon. He was a very handsome, charismatic, cutting edge kind of guy that both men and women seemed to want. And Jon loved everybody, literally everybody—Jon was bi, so when he walked into a room, he wanted everyone.

I had been doing readings for Jon for about six months. He liked me because I was blunt and to the point. I didn't know enough not to call him on his shit, and he seemed to get a kick out of that. When I would yell at him for being too self-absorbed or selfish he would laugh and ask me if I knew who he was. I would tell him just to shut up and listen, and he would just shake his head and say okay.

On this particular day, when I walked in to meet him, Jon was on the phone. He waved me in and I overheard him say to whomever he was talking to, "This is the guy I was talking about, you've got to talk to him," and then he handed me the phone.

I looked at Jon like "Who the fuck is this?" but he just motioned to talk to the person, so I did.

I said hello and the man on the other end said hello back. He said his name was Bob and that Jon really wanted me to talk to him. Right away I got bugged. I hated when people did this to me. It's like, "Wind up, monkey psychic, show me what you got" time, and I wasn't in the mood.

I sarcastically said, "Oh gee, that's great" and Bob started to laugh. I looked over at Jon and he too was smirking.

I decided not to be an asshole and go with it. I asked Bob how I could help him.

"I don't know," Bob said, "I don't know how this works."

"Well," I said, "I'm assuming you don't want to talk to me because I'm a nice guy, you probably want to ask a psychic question. So just ask me something and we can go from there." There was a pause and then Bob asked if his show was going to do well or not.

I gathered myself and concentrated on Bob. When I did, a whole new feeling came across me, an excited feeling. I had gotten excited about people in the past, when the information came in really clear or strong, or if I liked the person and what I was getting for them.

But this was different. It wasn't the information that had me excited, it was about Bob. I got excited about whatever Bob was doing, really excited. It felt like Christmas, that sense of anticipation. "Jesus, Bob," I said, "you got some seriously fun stuff coming up for you"

Bob laughed again. "Okay," he said, "what does that mean?"

I was so taken aback by this feeling, I didn't bother to figure out what it was about. It just felt big. I told him to give me a sec and I tried to ignore my excitement and concentrate on the logistics. All this information started coming like a flood. They talked about women, music, dancing, drugs. All sorts of categories, almost too much information.

"Who is this guy?" I kept asking myself. "What the hell is this feeling?" His initial question was easy—clearly the answer was yes, whatever show he was doing was going to be great—but I didn't want to let it go at that, I wanted to talk to this guy.

"Okay," I said, "you got some issues. You might cut things short sooner than you think, because you burn the candle at both ends *and* the middle. In fact, I'll be surprised if you make it through this call."

Bob went silent. I knew I was being dramatic, but as exciting as this guy was, there was also a feeling of danger around him. I could see how he was pushing things in all areas and I truly wasn't sure his heart was up to the task. But I knew if I said any more it would take the bite out of what I'd just said, so I held my tongue. Like in sales, you present your pitch and then shut up. First one to speak loses.

Finally Bob asked, "Are you being serious?" and I knew I had his attention. "No, Bob," I said, "I'm sure you'll make it through the call, but my lord, you've got this female spirit yelling at me to tell you to take it easy."

Again there was a pause and finally he said, "Really? That's interesting."

By now Jon was motioning to have the phone back, so I decided to wrap it up. "Okay Bob, let's review. YES on the show. Fifty-fifty on you being around to enjoy it."

"Okay," he said with a slight chuckle. "Nice talking to you, Michael."

"You too, Bob," I responded. And with that I handed the phone back to Jon.

I got up from the table to let those two talk without me around. I also needed to air out my head from talking to Bob.

That was amazing. His energy, his power. Whoever he was, I liked him. I could feel he wasn't a pushy man, but he didn't take the word no very easily. He knew what he wanted and that confidence, not cockiness, came through clearly.

I thought to myself, how was I going to talk to Jon now? There was such a difference in energy. I used to like to talk to Jon, he was cutting edge. But now it felt like I went from a tricycle to a chopper then back to the tricycle.

I walked back inside and Jon was still on the phone. He looked up and saw me. I heard him say, "Okay, he's back, I'll ask him and call you back," and hang up the phone. I went to the table and sat down. Jon looked happy.

"You made quite the impression on Bob," he said. "Did you figure out who he was?"

Now I was embarrassed. I didn't have a clue who this guy was, I just knew he wasn't your average guy. I suppose if I thought about it and put the pieces together, I might be able to guess in a month, but it wasn't like they said his name. In fact, they seemed to purposely not go there, like if I knew it might influence what I was getting. But I didn't want to tell Jon that, because it sounded like an excuse.

There's always a reason I don't pick up something about a person, something deeper and big-picture-like. But it always sounds like an excuse when I try to explain it, and the more you try to explain your reasoning, the worse you sound. I can hear the person think to themselves, "This guy is full of shit," and if I were sitting there listening to me, I'd think the same thing.

I told Jon I had no clue who he was and Jon shook his head "You call yourself a psychic?" he said. "That was Bob Fosse."

I got goosebumps; now it made sense. That feeling, that power.

I loved Bob Fosse. *All That Jazz* was one of my favorite movies. At Children's Theatre, where I briefly went to school, we studied Bob Fosse's techniques. He was a legend in the dance community. If I told my old instructor I talked to Bob Fosse, he'd pass out.

I tried to play it off like it was no big deal, but my stare suggested I was starstruck.

I asked Jon how he knew Bob Fosse, just to make sure I wasn't being played. He said they had met in New York some years back and they became friends. He said that Bob was so busy all the time they didn't talk much, but he called right after the last time Jon and I had chatted and Jon told Bob about the reading. He said Bob was curious, so he wanted to talk to me.

"He liked you," Jon said. "He liked how blunt you are."

"Well shit, next time you talk to him tell him I'd love to chat more," I said, and for the rest of the month I was on cloud nine. I wanted to tell everybody. I had talked to Bob fucking Fosse. Sure, we had only talked maybe a total of three minutes, but in my mind we were best buddies. It felt like I knew him, like really knew him. And how cool was that? I knew Bob Fosse.

I went to my mother's for dinner and I told her about talking to Bob Fosse. She wasn't impressed. Bob Hope, maybe! But Bob Fosse didn't hold any special meaning for her. I told her about *All That Jazz* and his amazing choreography, but she just kept peeling her potatoes and saying, "Oh that's nice, honey." Clearly my mother was crazy.

Finally, she stopped peeling and asked me what about this gentleman I found so interesting. I told her it was his energy, his power. I told her I had never felt that from someone before, and it was exciting. I had given readings to some local celebs and it was fun, but this was a whole new ball game. "Well maybe that's who you're supposed to work with honey," she said and asked me to help with the dinner.

I liked the thought of that. If I could get that vibe every time I did a reading? Hell yeah, I'd do that all day. "But how does one go about being a psychic to the stars?" I asked my mom. "It's not up to you honey," she calmly said. "It's up to Spirit. Just be available when they call and be yourself."

A week later I got a call from Jon. He wanted to know if I could talk to Bob again. "Of course," I said, and arrangements were made.

We started talking on a semi-regular basis, but the conversations were short, maybe ten minutes at a time. He would ask just one question at a time, like about his health or women.

He didn't like to get too deep into anything. If I started to elaborate, he would cut me short and say that's all he needed. He never paid me, and I never asked. That vibe was payment enough. I know it's important to get paid, self-worth, bills, and all of that, but sometimes the value is in the reading, and for me, talking to Bob was the value.

He started referring other people in the business to me. And like with Bob, they all brought that different vibration with them, that excitement.

It became harder for me to read "normal" people, and I started to see why the people who made it, made it.

I decided I needed to live in LA. I felt that just being around that energy would bring hope and excitement into my life.

So in 1984 I moved to Los Angeles with my buddy Stu.

We both had high hopes for our time there, new adventures, new opportunities. But the experience was a hard one for both of us. Stu would insist that it was much harder on him than me, but Stu's a bit off.

LA is a working town, a tough place to be unless you're employed or soon to be employed. The weather is amazing, the people watching is amazing. The clubs and nightlife were all where I wanted to be. But I couldn't get a job for the life of me. Stu, at least, got a job, from a guy I introduced him to. Me, I got nothing.

I had to come back with my tail between my legs, and go back to psychic readings. This was as depressing as it got for me. I remember seeing the Minneapolis skyline and thinking what a failure I was to have to come back.

But then, eleven years later, I was going back, and this time LA was asking me to come back. It felt like a second chance.

In 1995, I was approached by two producers from LA about the possibility of doing a movie based on my family and myself. They also asked about a possible television show spin-off.

Prior to this, my family and I had been on several shows, mostly about the novelty of a ghostbusting family and how we went about our daily lives.

One show even called us the world's most famous psychic family, which I thought was a tad over the top. Edina? Maybe. But the world? I wasn't sure about that. I know I didn't feel famous, but if it got the attention of people like Mimi and Diane, the producers who called, maybe I'd just shut my mouth and smile.

Mimi and Diane were both very strong women who came from different sides of the streets in LA. Mimi was all about films, having worked as a producer for several years on several films with A-list directors and actors, and from what I read, doing so very successfully.

Diane was from the television side of things. She had worked on several successful series, and was well-liked and respected. For some reason, I trusted them both.

The two had joined forces. They both worked for other people, but wanted to step out on their own. They had other projects going, but seemed excited to work with me.

The plan was to have me come out to LA, meet with the different studios, meet with writers, come up with a script, and eventually get a movie done.

The pitch was *The Wonder Years* meets *The Addams Family*. They were excited, I was excited. I signed the contracts and off I went.

There's a thing about Hollywood—the community is made up of circles. The outer circle is where the wannabes live. The dreamers waiting to be discovered, the writers just hoping for their first break, the students dying to be seen.

There's the inner circle. You have to be invited into that circle, welcomed. People in that circle are very protective. They know how hard it is to get into that circle, and they guard it with their lives. You can sometimes be born into that circle, but you still have to perform. If you're just a sibling, you can stay in the circle, but you have to eat at the kids table.

People in that circle like to keep it small; some people are kicked out.

If you prove yourself worthy, they will ask you back in, but rarely do they ask twice.

And then there's an even smaller circle that very few people are in. You have to do some serious shit to get in this circle. This circle is where the real movers and shakers are. They get things done at BBQs and AA meetings. It's all about relationships. Getting an edge, having power.

The one thing that will kill you in Hollywood is desperation. People can smell it, it stinks. And if you're desperate, you're not allowed to stay in the inner circle.

When I came back in '95, I was given a pass to the inner circle. I wasn't allowed to stay, and chances are I'd be forgotten ten minutes after I left, but while I was relevant, I could hang.

For ten years I got to stay, and I loved almost every minute of it.

One of the first things I noticed was that a lot of what went on in the movies would actually happen in real life. For instance, if a couple were romantically involved in a film, they "practiced" a lot between takes. Even if they were married or engaged or going steady, it was considered work.

Where people would ask for my help was when the filming was over and they wrapped the show. In some cases, the couple never really heard the word "cut."

Another one I would get a lot of calls about were professional relationships. Would this director work well with this actor? Would this producer get that writer? What person would work better in different situations?

Then there were the constant questions about change—actors wanted to direct, directors wanted to act. Producers wanted showrunners, showrunners wanted that "thing." And writers just didn't want to be thrown out with the garbage.

Writers had it tough in Hollywood. In my mind, they brought the most, but were treated the worst. I don't think ever in the history of Hollywood did a writer write a script and have it stay the same throughout the whole production. Everybody pees on the tree in that town, but it sure kept me working.

Once I got past the fact that I was talking to one of my favorite performers, it was easy work.

But that was another part of that world that was fascinating. Many times, the person I watched on screen was the complete opposite in real life.

The tough guys were the pushovers, the weak ones were the tough guys.

The friendly, happy-go-lucky types in film were complete assholes when the cameras were off and the assholes on film couldn't be kinder.

It appeared the more successful you were, the less of diva you'd become. The real big dogs were very approachable, once you got through their buffers.

It was the world of make-believe, my favorite place. The creativity, and the belief that what they were doing was more real than real life, made my job fun.

Even the ghosts were easier there.

One of my favorite people in the world is my friend Donna. Mimi introduced us within the first few weeks of me getting to know Mimi. I gave Donna a reading and we became fast friends.

Donna is a former Miss North Carolina, a true beauty queen, but only in appearance. Donna is just as comfortable riding a four-wheeler and tearing up the yard as she is wearing an evening gown and walking the red carpet. She's tough, smart, and one of the kindest people I know.

She was married to Tony Scott, director of *Top Gun*, *Days of Thunder*, *Beverly Hills Cop II*, *Enemy of the State*, and so many more. Tony was the kind of guy who made you feel welcome, no matter who you were. He barely knew me, yet he welcomed me into his home and never made me feel unwanted.

When we would go out to eat, actors, producers, and other directors would flock to him in hopes of kissing the ring. A-list actors would get silly talking to him, and he was always gracious. He was a very loved man, even his crew would follow him from film to film.

They lived on the top of Benedict Canyon, high above Beverly Hills, in what was known as the Barrymore Estate.

The Barrymore Estate was called that because the previous owner was John Barrymore. And according to legend, wild parties were the norm back then. So wild, in fact, that there was talk of deadly malfeasance. And because of that, the guest house was haunted.

Besides all the other talents Donna has, she's also very sensitive to spirits. She asked me if I could get rid of the spirits in her guest house, and of course I agreed to help.

Donna's house was something right out of central casting. A beautiful Spanish-style home built into the hills, with a waterfall pool, lush lawn, and panoramic view that let you literally see from downtown LA to the ocean and beyond.

The air was thick with the smell of night-blooming jasmine, the century-old trees guarded the grounds and muted the sounds of the city a mile down the hill.

It felt calm and nostalgic. Phone numbers for Charlie Chaplin and Douglas Fairbanks were still on the wall in the phone room. It was like stepping back in time.

The property included the main house—with an office Tony used separate from the house—and a guesthouse, which was also separate.

It was in the two-story, two-bedroom guest house that Donna noticed most of the activity.

I *had* felt the presence of someone, but that was the extent of it. No real activity, no lights going on and off, no cold air. Just the heaviness of somebody not happy at my being there.

Sometimes spirits don't like to show themselves to me because they just want me to go away. That's what this felt like.

But sometimes Spirit will show up for someone not used to dealing with ghosts, someone who might not take the whole subject that seriously. And I had the perfect guy in mind.

One of my best buddies in LA was a guy named Daniel. He lived in Silver Lake, a hip, artistic kind of place, near downtown. Daniel and I hung out a lot on my trips to LA; in fact I stayed with him often when I was out there. He was also a director, having moved to LA from Minneapolis after the success of his first film.

Daniel wasn't that into the psychic stuff, though he had some experience with it earlier in his life and even knew Birdie. But he was more a "wait and see" kind of guy. Perfect for what I needed on this particular job.

I told Daniel that I was going to do a ghostbusting for Donna.

He liked Donna. I introduced them on one of my trips out west and they both got along. He was also a fan of Tony. It all sounded intriguing, so he agreed to come.

The plan was that Daniel and I would sleep in the guest house. We had checked it out earlier, but so far there had been no activity. We thought if we slept there, we might piss off whoever was haunting the place and we could start the busting, even if it was really late.

We hung out with Donna until about two in the morning. Tony was working so we had the place to ourselves.

On the outside, the guest house had that cozy cabin vibe to it. But it was no cabin. Like everything else on the property, they spared no expense. From the beds to the lighting, it had more of a five-star hotel feel inside. We wouldn't be slumming it. Daniel took the room upstairs, I took the room downstairs.

I settled in rather nicely. I was a little curious if something was going to happen when I fell asleep, but that bed was so nice that I wasn't sure I'd care.

Daniel, on the other hand, was having a rougher night. He tried to lay down, but he felt the presence of a female in the room. He went to the bathroom to gather his thoughts and splash some water on his face. When he went to the bathroom, he looked in the mirror and saw a woman in the reflection, looking back at him.

This didn't exactly settle Daniel down. The next thing I know, Daniel's waking me up with a "holy shit" look on his face, asking me to move over.

I love Daniel; I'd take a bullet for him, like in the arm or maybe the leg. Not a groin shot, but I'd definitely take a foot shot. But I wasn't sure I wanted to sleep with him, especially with him sweating the way he was.

I know we agreed that if we saw a spirit we would do the busting, but I was totally not in the mood anymore. I just wanted to go back to sleep. So I suggested he stay there and I would sleep upstairs. He seemed comfortable with that plan, so we switched rooms.

When I went upstairs, besides every light being on, I noticed that there was something different in the room. It didn't feel scary or threatening, just active.

I turned off the lights and settled in again. I heard some rustling noises in the bathroom, but whatever it was could come to me. I wasn't going to chase anything, I was tired.

Right when I closed my eyes, I could tell something was in the room. I opened my eyes and sure enough, a woman dressed like a flapper was standing at the foot of my bed.

Maybe it was the setting, maybe it was the night-blooming jasmine, but it just didn't bother me to see her. She was visibly upset with our presence and she was clear as a bell, which meant she was a strong spirit. But I found myself thinking like a surfer after a couple of Buds. I almost called her dude.

I told her to chill, to relax, but this only made her look more upset. I told her I wasn't here to upset her, but to see if we could find a way to get her to cross to the other side. She was having none of it.

She said she hated men, especially the one downstairs (Daniel). She said she wanted us both gone, and unless we left, she was going to haunt us.

I couldn't help but laugh. I had been around mean, evil, rotten, stinking ghosts for most of my life. But when she threatened to haunt us, it struck me as cute, like when your eight-year-old threatens to run away.

My reaction to her threat was the last straw. She left, and with her, that feeling of her presence in the room. Now it felt normal and comfortable again.

I snuggled in and relaxed. I started to doze off, when again I was awoken by a white and sweaty Daniel. "Move over," he said, "I'm not sleeping alone."

I asked him what was wrong. He told me he fell asleep, but then something moved his bed. He opened his eyes and the flapper was standing right over him. He said he freaked out and came upstairs.

There was no other room to move to and it was too late to wake up Donna to see if we could sleep in the main house, so I agreed to let him sleep with me and we settled in.

I wasn't worried about the flapper coming back; she didn't want a thing to do with me. Now my concern was with Daniel—what if he snored or got the jimmies?

The next day, I told Donna what happened the night before and the issues the spirit had with men. She didn't flinch. In fact, she seemed relieved. I asked her if she wanted to force the issue and get her to go away permanently, but she seemed okay with having her stay awhile.

That was fine with me. I was still in awe of my surroundings and something about it being so beautiful made getting rid of a ghost feel less urgent.

I found that to be true about all the ghostbusting jobs I did out in LA

The ghosts were just as mean, but when I looked outside and the place was so alive, I couldn't blame them for wanting to stay. In Minnesota, with our winter weather, cloudy skies, and depressing landscapes, it's like you're doing them a favor by escorting them to the other side. Here? Hang ten, dude, ride the wave.

On the negative side of LA is the shallowness. Talent is important and a lot of successful people are there because they worked hard and never quit, but a large part of success is also luck and timing.

Some of the people I worked with got lucky and they became famous quickly, before they could handle it. And in their minds, maybe they didn't feel like they deserved all the accolades. But instead of just being honest about that, they believed they must be special and they became entitled divas.

Whatever hole they have inside they cover up with how loved they are, how popular they are, how important they are.

I believe we all have holes. I haven't met a person yet who doesn't have a hole in their soul, an empty spot. That rush of success in Hollywood that some of those people get covers all of those holes. They forget that fame *temporarily* covers those holes. When the rush is over, reality comes back.

There's where all the drugs and alcohol come into play.

When I was young, I was very direct, almost dark at times. In Hollywood, this approach worked the best. I tried to take the high road at times, but most of the time the people I talked too were so used to getting smoke blown up their asses that they didn't listen to the positive spin.

I did a reading for this actor who had done several films in the '80s and was from a well-known acting family. When I opened up psychically on him, I could tell he needed some hope. His acting career was winding down, he was more interested in directing than acting, and he just felt down.

I decided not to concentrate on the negative. I told him about all the positive things that were coming for him, all the possibilities. He had a really supportive spouse, which wasn't the case for a lot of people I read. He was very creative and connected. And it just felt like all he needed to do was not give up and he would be okay.

At the end, I asked if any of it made sense. He said it did, but he was disappointed because he felt I was too positive. I was speechless. He continued.

He went on to say that he didn't want a reading of the possibilities, he wanted a real reading, not fluff.

I wasn't used to someone accusing me of being fluffy. I was a little put off that he didn't see the value of what I was trying to tell him.

He started to walk away and I called him back. In my mind, there are many different realities; it's up to you which one you want. And if this little asshole wanted *that* reality, I was more than willing to oblige.

I told him I forgot a few things. I told him his life was going to suck, he wasn't going to get the job he was hoping for, and his money was going to run out. I told him his ego was so large that nobody was going to work with him again. I suggested he move to Europe and start over.

I suggested that even though his wife was supportive now, that she was going to tire of his whiny attitude and leave him.

I smiled and reminded him that the only reason he was even in this business was because his father was a successful actor. And it was my opinion that he didn't deserve any of the success he'd had.

I asked him if he understood what I said and he looked at me in amazement. "Now *that* was a reading," he said and asked if he could call me again. I told him he couldn't afford me and I walked away. He called me for months afterward. Some people love the dark stuff.

Please don't get me wrong, I don't believe people in the entertainment business are better than the people who aren't. I don't. There are some real assholes in that business. But there's a reason I love working with them.

And it's not just the people in the business that are affected by success, I've seen it in psychics out there as well.

I went to a lot of different meetings in LA. I went to pitch meetings. That's where you pitch your idea for your film or series and hope somebody picks it up. I also went to a lot of meetings where the people at the studios wanted me or someone like me to do a show.

Those meetings were my least favorites, because I was always asked to do readings or show them something that they thought viewers would find interesting. Wind-up monkey kind of thing. I didn't do well in those type of meetings. I'd snarl and growl.

On one particular trip I had been in LA for about a month. My manager called Sunday night and said he set up a huge meeting at one of the studios for the next day. I was scheduled to go home Tuesday, and I was spent. Life for me in LA was nonstop. I told him I was going to pass. I had packing and goodbyes to do and I really wasn't in the mood. As managers do, he insisted, telling me this could be the big one and I would kick myself if some other psychic got the job just because I wasn't in the mood.

He reminded me that if I did get this show, it would help all the other things I was doing. He could sell my movie idea easier if I was on a reality show.

I gave in and the next day we both went to the studio.

I was in Studio City, my manager was in Beverly Hills, and the meeting was in Burbank. I suggested that I could just meet him at the studio, because for me it was just over the hill, but he wanted to go over a few things before we went in. So of course we were late.

When we walked into the room where everyone had gathered, at least a dozen other psychics were all siting at a large table discussing what they could bring to a show, if hired.

Also in the room were the producers, eagerly listening and lapping up all the suggestions that were being made.

Everyone stopped talking when we entered the room. One of the producers said, "Oh good, we're all here," and pointed to two empty chairs for us to sit in.

A quick look around the room and I could see it was a pretty eclectic group. There were a couple of old-school psychics, confident, but bored with the proceedings; a few more regular psychics; and of course the newbies, gushing because they got asked to come, doing all the talking because they clearly had more to offer.

Introductions had already been made, so the producer who showed us to our seats asked that we introduce ourselves to the group.

I introduced myself, along with my manager. One of the newbies asked what I had done, and I told her I wasn't sure what she meant. She asked what kind of shows I had been on.

I instantly hated her.

"Oh," I said, "let's see…my first show was, of course, *Romper Room*. The grab bags were fabulous. I tried to get on *Sesame Street*, but you know politics."

My manager, Steve, grabbed my hand and interrupted me. "Michael's being…nevermind." Then he went on to do an oral resume of all the things I'd done and the famous people I'd read.

It's an awkward thing when someone does that while you're sitting there. It seemed like the norm out there, but I never got used to it.

After he finished, smiles were seen throughout the room. Not "wow, we're impressed" smiles, but "okay, he's cool" smiles.

One of the producers caught us up on what they were thinking. He said they were discussing a possible show where a group of us would go around and do readings for people on the spot. They were looking for the right types.

He asked me if I was able to pick up things quickly, like on the spot.

I said, "You mean can I pick up that you're seeing your best friend's sister on the side, even though you're married? That fast?"

Again, Steve grabbed my hand and interrupted. "Yes," he said with an apologetic smile. "Yes, that's not an issue." Then he switched the attention from me and the now-uncomfortable producer, to the others in the group.

"What experience have you guys had?" Now everybody was uncomfortable.

Steve was great.

The newbie who asked who I was spoke first. "Well I think that's very inappropriate, I don't want to be involved with that kind of show." Another producer started to explain that it wasn't going to be that kind of show, when one of the older psychics chimed in, "That's because you're not ready, dear, you're just starting out."

The newbie got upset, and she started listing all the famous people who come to her. She'd have us know she wasn't just starting out, she had been doing this at least a year and was very gifted.

Another psychic took offense. She suggested that the newbie was edgy because she needed a drink. She did feel like she wanted to get a drink before the leprechauns showed up.

Now everybody was talking. One was trying to convince the producers that she was just as fast as I was, another one agreed with the older one about the newbie needing a drink.

Things really heated up when another psychic suggested that the pay should be based on years of experience and accuracy.

It felt like a street fight between the Jets and the Sharks; the only thing missing was the music.

I kept my mouth shut. It was fun just watching it all play out. Besides, I knew when I walked in that the only thing I was going to get out of this was the free water they gave us when we showed up.

Nothing really came of the hundreds of meetings and hundreds of people I've met so far, but now I don't take as seriously as I did in my twenties.

Between my family and myself, we must have shot a dozen sizzles: ten- to thirteen-minute videos of the wacky, wonderful world of the Bodines.

Producers shop them around and hope a studio will pick it up.

And then there are the producers looking for the novelty approach.

We've done *Psychics in the Kitchen*, where Echo and I did a talk show answering the studio audience's psychic questions. *Street Psychics*, where I would go up to people on the street and answer any psychic question they might have.

Shopping with a Psychic, *Mowing with a Psychic*, *Bowling with a Psychic*. Anything they could think of that they thought would sell.

Some of the show ideas these people come up with are embarrassing. I had one producer suggest I let my son get possessed so I could show how to do an exorcism. Another group wanted to set up a psychic competition, like *Star Search* or *The Voice.*

At one pitch meeting, I suggested they dress a psychic up in a bacon suit and put them at one end of a cage with a key just a few feet above their heads. On the other end, put a starving, drooling, crazed lion. With each correct psychic question and answer, the key would be lowered closer to the cage. With each incorrect answer, a separator would be removed from the cage.

You could call it *Guess What's for Dinner.*

If they're good, they get to move on; if not, you thin the herd. "Win, win," I said.

It took them three full minutes to decide it was a bad idea.

I do love that town.

THE POINT

In December 2002, everything was going okay. My wife, Kate, and I had been married for fifteen years. The salon she owned for most of our marriage was booming. My amazing kids, ages ten and twelve at the time, were in school and having fun. I was still a stay-at-home dad, watching the kids, working on my first book, and doing readings for the occasional celeb. But something was off.

The winters in Minnesota are brutal. People around here go to Siberia to warm up. You have to get away or you end up going mental—or worse, ice fishing. Our plan was to spend New Year's someplace warmer, and since I don't fly, we decided to take a road trip to our timeshare in Daytona Beach, Florida.

We had done this a couple times before and let me tell you, it's not an easy trip with two kids and a dog driving all the way to Florida in a minivan. It's not just the port-a-potty after a chili and popcorn cook-off smell that you can *never* get out of the car. It's the lack of leg room and movement that makes you pray for an early death. Your legs hurt, your butt hurts, you look like hell. Every time we'd come back from one of those trips, we'd swear to God we'd never do it again. My kids considered it child abuse.

But this year I had a plan. This year we were going to go cross-country in style and luxury, this year I was renting a Winnebago.

My first clue that I was about to embark on the trip from hell should have been the luck I had in finding a thirty-five-foot Winnebago at the first place I called. My father always said, "When you play poker, never win the first hand. The gods see you don't need luck because you already have it and you lose your shirt by morning." I was told by just about everyone that knew these sort of things that finding a Winnebago to rent this close after Christmas, without reserving it six months in advance, was going to be nearly impossible.

But there I was talking to Winnebago Bob about his brand new thirty-five-foot Winnie Sunstar that just arrived that day, and how lucky I was to be the first caller to get it.

Had I ever driven a thirty-five-footer before? Bob wanted to know. "Of course I have," I replied, "I've driven much bigger ones in the past, Bob, but I just love those little thirty-five-footers," I said, lying through my teeth.

"Ah, great then," Bob said, "you're going to love this one, brand new, not a scratch on her."

"Great, Bob," I replied, "just the way I like 'em."

And then, as I hung up the phone, and my fake smile slowly disappeared, the reality of the conversation hit me. I'd never driven a thirty-five-foot Winnebago before, was it big? Was it thick? I saw old people driving them all the time. How hard could it be? Besides, I drive the hell out of our minivan; I own the road in that puppy. How many times have I driven a U-Haul across the country? Three times? And nobody died during those trips. And with new modern technology, I bet they practically drove themselves.

Winnebago Bob's wasn't exactly across the street; in fact I'm not sure it was even in my state. But the drive out to boonyville gave me a chance to rehearse my best "howdy Bob, where's the buttermilk" attitude, which I knew I'd need when renting a thirty-five-foot Winnie Sunstar for the first time. First impressions are important; my fear was that Bob would see through my casual, calm demeanor and let someone else rent the new Winnie. Or worse, charge me a "he looks like a psychic" fee when I was already barely able to make the deposit. So I cranked up the country music, put my hair in a baseball cap, and tried to channel the nearest dead truck driver I could find.

I finally made my way through the cornfields and the waste deposit plants and arrived at Winnebago Bob's shortly before closing. This turned out to be perfect timing because WB was more interested in getting home to his little parts than checking me out. He met me at the door with the contracts and pen in hand, anxious to get that $2,000 deposit we had discussed earlier on the phone. "Did you bring cash?" he asked as he searched for the keys. "Yup," I replied and I handed him the rolled-up twenties and c-notes I'd been saving since forever. "Good, good," he answered back and quickly counted what I had just given him.

It was as he counted the last hundred that he actually looked at me for the first time. I smiled, he paused and gave me the once over. "Did we discuss insurance?" he asked with a weird look. "We sure did, Bob," I replied. "We are covered." The spring came back to his step.

He smiled. "That's great, just great. Okay, she's out back. Here are the keys, you can leave your car in the lot, and we'll see you in ten days."

With that, Winnebago Bob put the $2,000 in cash in his pocket, pointed to what looked like a small school on wheels, and started out the door to show me. "Wow, she's a beaut," I said, trying to hold back my shock.

"Oh yeah, she's something," he replied, as he put on his coat and searched for the keys. "And remember," he said, "not a scratch on her." He put out his hand, dropped the keys into mine, slapped my shoulder, and said, "Have a good trip, Mr. Bodine."

As I pulled out of Bob's I was surprised at how well the Winnie handled. Granted, I didn't have to back up or do a sharp turn, but it felt easy to drive and light for a thirty-five-footer.

I showed Kate and the kids the Winnebago and the kids got excited. All the gear was packed and ready to go, so it was just a matter of putting it all in the Winnie and hitting the road. Kate was a bit freaked out. "That's huge," she said and I of course looked at my crotch and said thank you. She gave me an "oh please" look and we headed out of town, excited, optimistic, and ready to leave the grey and cold behind.

Our plan was to stay ahead of a storm front that was moving through Illinois. In order to do this, we had to go through Wisconsin in six hours. Normally it takes eight, but I figured since we only had to stop for gas because we had everything we needed in the Winnie, we might be able to shave off an hour or two and be ahead of the storm. But as things go, that didn't happen, and by the time we got to northern Illinois we were in a full-fledged blizzard.

We were about five miles away from our first stop, Mattoon, Illinois. We had stopped there on our last trip. It was a cute little town with all the things you need when you're traveling cross-country. The hotel we stayed in when we last went through had hook-ups for RVs, and I was excited to spend our first night in the camper.

We were slowly making our way through Illinois. If you've ever traveled through the great state of Illinois, you know that the highways tend to be slightly elevated from the corn fields and alfalfa farms. This, I'm told, helps with drainage during thunderstorms or prevents wildlife from casually walking across a busy highway. But not so great if you add a trace of snow and a touch of wind. Throw in a blizzard, like the one that followed us from our home state of Minnesota, and it's downright dangerous.

By now traffic was at a crawl. The storm was in full force. I passed several cars in the ditch as we got closer to Mattoon. I thought to myself, "How stupid do you have to be to get stuck in a ditch, especially when you're on a straight road?" Just about the time I was thinking that, the road curved sharply to the left. A cop with a flashlight was pointing traffic in the direction of the road, but the Winnie was having none of it. Instead of turning left, she decided she wanted to go straight, so headfirst we plowed into the deep snow ten feet past the road. As we did, I noticed the cop do the olé with his hands like a matador does to a charging bull, and I heard Kate yell, "HERE WE GO! HERE WE GO!"

When we finally stopped, we were waist high in a snow bank. The front end was buried to the point that you couldn't see the headlights anymore. Snow was halfway up the front window and the back end was sticking out.

I asked if everybody was okay and they were. No scratches or bruises, just shock. The cop knocked on the door and asked if we were okay. We struggled to open the door, and when we opened it up he peered in. "Come on folks," he said, "I'll drive you into town." We gathered our things and headed out to the squad car. When I got out and looked at the RV, it was clear we weren't going to get out on our own.

After he got off the radio, letting someone know he was bringing us in, the first thing he said was, "I thought you people from Minnesota knew how to drive in these conditions."

To which Kate goes into the whole, "This is the first time my husband has driven an RV and normally he knows what he's doing" monologue. I wasn't there; I was in the back, staring out the window, wishing we had flown.

The next two days we spent arranging a tow, going back and forth to the RV, and enjoying the warm hospitality of Mattoon.

Finally, on day three and nine hundred dollars later, we were ready to leave. There was some damage to the Winnie, but nothing a little glue or duct tape wouldn't fix.

For the next two days, my hands were so tight on the steering wheel that my knuckles were literally white. My head was playing tricks on me. It felt like the RV was floating all over the road. I kept seeing us going into another ditch, and now we were in mountain country. I wasn't worried about going up, it was the coming down that had me freaked. And guess what? The storm had hit there too. Everywhere was wet, slippery, and steep.

Needless to say, the trip now had a different feel. The adventure vibe was replaced with a survival vibe. The mood in the RV was tense. Kate was mad because we weren't going to spend New Year's in Florida; we celebrated in some back-water town outside of Atlanta. The cold weather had made its way south, so even when we finally did arrive, it was going to be unseasonably cold. All our extra cash was gone, I was going to have to have someone wire us some.

Everything about this trip kept getting worse and worse. When we finally got to our timeshare, I pulled into the building, knocking off all the fancy, newly installed overhanging lights in the front entrance. Ting, Ting, Ting, Ting. They all popped off. Hoping nobody noticed, I tried backing up, but I almost went through a brick wall. Thank God the now-dented bumper stopped me.

We couldn't just drive to a restaurant, no place to park. We couldn't swim because it was freezing outside. We had no money to do anything fun, and even our dog Harry was bummed and bored.

Kate kept insisting we go to the lighthouse at the other end of the peninsula. I didn't want to go, because I didn't want to drive that damn RV anywhere. But by the end of the stay her "if we don't do something other than sit in this timeshare, I'm going to kill you" talk had worn me down.

Off we went. It was around four o'clock in the afternoon when we left. We didn't think about traffic because we were too busy hating each other. According to the pamphlet, the lighthouse closed at five, so time was a factor. But just like how everything went on that trip, we were stuck.

I couldn't suggest we not go, because I still needed my testicles. If I drove slow, Kate would know I was stalling and life would equate to being in hell with a toothache. My only option was to get there any way I could, and get there fast.

Forty-five minutes of "take this road, no take that one, don't miss the light" and finally we had reached our destination. By this time, Kate and I loathed each other. The trip, the crash, the weather, the RV. We were done.

I suggested I'd take Harry for a walk and she could take the kids to the lighthouse. I got no argument.

I grabbed the leash and the dog and off we went down the dirt road that got us there. About a half a block down I saw what looked like an abandoned road to my left. The trees lined the road, and as we went further, the trees got thicker and thicker. It was now dusk, the sun was setting, and a warm, soft light was filling the trees. I saw some houses up ahead, so I knew people must use this road. Still, it had an old feeling to it.

Further down the road, I smelled burning wood. I assumed someone in one of the houses had built a fire. It smelled nice, mixed with the cool air and the soft light, and I felt myself calming down from the drive. Then I heard singing, first faint and then, as I walked toward it, strong. It was happy sounding, just an accordion and some men singing old pirate songs.

Harry heard them too, and he stuck his nose up in the air to smell whoever was there. We were getting closer to the singing. To my left I saw a black cast-iron fence surrounding an unkempt yard. Inside the cast-iron fence I saw the men sitting around a fire, dressed in gear you'd see in the 1800s.

It looked at first like they were having a block party, but their clothes looked so authentic. We stopped and listened. Harry barked once, but I pulled on his leash to stop, so he just growled a bit. They didn't take notice of us; they just kept playing and laughing. By now it was getting dark.

On the other side of the street was an old house, but it looked like nobody was home. I wondered if they knew these people.

Suddenly, I got this overwhelming feeling. *I* knew these people. One of them, wearing pirate's gear with black and white striped knee-high socks, looked at me and motioned for me to come toward them. Then they all looked at me. I knew this man, I knew these people. They were my friends, I could smell the sea on them, and it all felt like home.

As one of them came closer to me, he was smiling. I could smell the rum on his breath. Harry started to bark again. I looked down to tell him to stop, but when I looked up, they were gone. Poof.

I could still hear the faint sound of music, but that too eventually went away.

They only things there were several old gravestones, littered within the fence. In the middle was a stone plaque, overgrown with plants, that read, "Dedicated to men who served under Ponce de León."

I've never been that much into past lives, never saw the reason to be. I have enough trouble just getting through this life. But I *know* I was one of those men, I could feel it in my soul. I know I was a pirate. I wasn't a great pirate, probably a deckhand of some kind, but that was my life.

Somehow seeing them changed everything. I understood why I struggle the way I do, why I think the way I do. It was a hard life back then, misery was commonplace, but so was laughing and drinking and fighting and adventure. I missed that smell, that fun. I could feel the sea and the wind, and I knew who I was.

By the time Harry and I made it back to the lighthouse, I was flying. I had never experienced anything like that before and I felt great.

Kate was still sour—the lighthouse closed before they let her climb to the top and basically it was my fault—but I didn't care. She could have blamed me for the Kennedy assassination and I wouldn't have cared.

The rest of the trip was a blur. I was so excited by my experience that I didn't care about the drive back or explaining to Winnebago Bob why his new Winnie came back looking like it went off a cliff. It just didn't matter. The crash didn't matter, the driving, the cold, the fighting, nothing mattered. The whole trip was worth it.

Answers come. Even when you hate everybody and everything, they come. If you're cynical, it doesn't matter; they come. Not looking? They come. And when they do, all the crap you had to go through to get them doesn't matter anymore either.

CONCLUSION

Chapter 1

In the first chapter, I talked about psychics. The reason I talked about psychics was to plant a seed. I wanted to point out that yes, we can be a bit strange, we can be territorial or dramatic. We can be judgmental and ego-driven. We can be fake, we can be phony. But we can also be right. Go to a bunch of psychics and ask them the same question. Chances are you'll get the same response, just presented in different ways.

And if we can be right, what does that mean? It means there's something else out there. It means maybe it's real.

If life isn't about making money and scoring toys, what's it about? Maybe everything we go through happens for a reason, maybe you're reading this book for a reason. Maybe that's the point of chapter one.

But let me ask you something. Do you really think that psychics who charge a lot and dress in costumes are better than ones who don't? Or if a psychic is on TV, does that make them better than the psychics who aren't?

Because I'm here to tell you, they're not.

Please stop being so closed-minded. Maybe it's fear, maybe the whole concept is just too much for you to bear, so you make fun of it. But I'll try to keep it simple for you folks that have a hard time with it: psychic not bad, psychic good.

Chapter 2

The point of chapter 2 is to show you that answers come from all sorts of places, not just psychics. They come to us every day, in small ways and big. It starts with trusting yourself, trusting that inner voice. Don't just sit and ask, do something—anything.

Action and movement is the key. The best way to get answers is to act. You hate your job? That in itself is an answer. If you're sick of your job, that's different, welcome to the club. I swear there are days when I just can't take another possession. But if you *hate* your job, do something. Volunteer at a place you like, take a class you're interested in, walk a different path than you normally take. Answers will come! Just change it up a little.

If you're too cynical or afraid to try something, wait until they make your situation unbearable or you get sick, then try something, and not just something lateral. If you really hate your life, remember that you put yourself there.

Maybe you didn't think it was going to be this bad or you thought you were doing the right thing. But you *can* take yourself out. It's all about belief and intent. Try it, just try doing something else that you think you might like. Watch how new people and new opportunities come to you.

Chapter 3

The takeaway from chapter 3 is that we all have guides that love us and are around us all the time. Not your friends or relatives, but higher souls and higher energy. Ones that don't care that we go to the bathroom or have sex, but just want us happy.

You don't have to believe me. I didn't believe it either, at first. But I believe it now. I believe it because of what other people have said to me and because of what I've seen. It's comforting, especially when I feel alone or sad.

Use your guides and don't blame them for the problems you have. Use them to get out of your problems. That's why they're around. They're gifts.

Chapter 4

Chapter 4 basically reminds you that death sucks. I'm a psychic and I hate it; I hate losing people I love. But the dead do come to us, in dreams, through mediums, or in person. They can't always stick around because they have places to be and staying here would be too painful, for them and for you. But they don't really die, they just move on.

But here's the other point: You're still alive and people you love are still alive. When people die, you don't have the chance to tell them how much you loved them and how much they helped you. Use this opportunity to tell people that you love how important they are to you and why they are important to you.

One of the biggest regrets the dead have is that they didn't appreciate and tell the people they loved how they felt when they were alive. You're alive. Don't take that for granted, use it.

Another regret the dead have are the missed opportunities or the unnecessary worry over money, time, or being liked. Who cares? You're alive! Most of the spirits I talk to would give anything for just one more day! Yet we go decades without doing anything better for ourselves.

It's game over when you die, at least for your body.

Chapter 5

Chapter 5's point was that you have power over ghosts and you can deal with them yourself. If you still think I'm crazy or the thirty-five million people who claim to have had a ghostly experience are crazy, fuck you, you're an idiot.

At the very least, have an open mind. If you don't see or feel them, but one of your family members or friends does, don't torment them with your ignorance. Listen to them.

You won't look weak or stupid if you listen to them. You'll look strong and caring. You'll look like an asshole if it turns out you really have a ghost, I promise you that.

Chapter 6

Chapter 6 was about reality and fantasy and how thin that line can be. People say to me, "Well in reality, blah blah blah ..." I say there are many realities. One man's ceiling is another man's floor. Open your mind!

Go to a psychic if you want, but answers will come regardless. But don't just sit and think, "Oh my life sucks." Boo-fucking-hoo! Move! Just do something. It doesn't have to be big. Guides need movement, they need action.

If you have a dream, that's even better. And if you have a vision, fuck, you're practically there. Let guides show you, like they showed me.

And do me a favor and cut psychics some slack. Do you know how weird it is to be a psychic? Today I went shopping. I passed by a guy and I saw this movie of him in my head, how he's going to be a successful athlete and then blow out his left knee. They showed me his X-rays! They also showed me the cashier's eating disorder and the bag boy's crush on the manager.

I hear stuff all the time!

And I see ghosts all the time too. I stopped caring whether people had skin or were alive long ago. I assume everybody's dead!

I walk by people who are about to die or get sick. I hear peoples' thoughts and fears. It's constant.

You know when you round a corner and you bump into a person? I turn the corner and there's a ghost standing there looking at me! Try having that experience at two in the morning when you're alone.

There was a time when none of this would have mattered. I was six! If I saw a ghost, I'd wet my pants and run away! Problem solved.

But things happen, coincidences occur. And it's impossible to run away.

What's the Point?

Minneapolis in the '80s was a hotbed for comedic talent and acting.

Places like the Guthrie, Mixed Blood, the Children's Theatre, and Old Log were attracting all kinds of talent. Louie Anderson, Mo Collins, Al Franken, and Pat Kroft all came from that time and that place. The town had a feeling of creativity to it. For me, one of the main spots for creative, cutting edge comedy and acting was a place called Dudley Riggs's Brave New Workshop. Dudley's was a sketch comedy improvisation theatre that had been around since the '60s. They put on shows, usually with a political theme, nine times a week, Tuesday through Saturday, and did improv after the shows on Saturdays.

I worked at the theatre in my early twenties. Not as an actor, I didn't have the chops. I took tickets, worked concessions, swept up, basic Gilligan stuff. The money wasn't great, Dudley was known to be a tad tight with a buck, but the benefits of being around and learning from some of the best performers I had ever seen was priceless to me.

I had gone to the Children's Theatre, I took classes at the Guthrie. But this place was different. The actors were fast, funny, and smart; they made the *Saturday Night Live* crew look like the cast of *Full House*. Every night, they seemed to kill, and every chance I got, I watched. They didn't care if they offended anybody, they actually seemed to like it if they did. They danced with each other with words and actions, they challenged each other to be better, to not be lazy. If they fucked up, they made it a part of the show. No one actor tried to outshine the others, and watching them was like watching a ballet. They flowed. One of the best actors, as far as I was concerned, was a guy named Jeff Gadbois.

I didn't know Jeff. I think the only words he spoke to me were, "Hey asshole, get back here, it's fucking intermission." (Long story. I saw my ex walk by with a guy and I kinda left.) But I watched him, I studied him. This guy could think lightning fast. He could change characters in an instant. He wasn't just funny, he was smart funny; he didn't just make you laugh, he made you think. I would watch the audience whenever I knew he would talk because I loved looking at their reactions. I was in awe of this guy.

I learned a lot of things back then about people, comedy, and how each audience is different. But one of the two big things I learned was that talent wasn't always rewarded. People like Mark Bergren, Chris Dent, and Jeff Gadbois should have been household names, but they're not. I realized that talent is only a small part of what makes a person famous. In some cases, you don't even need that. Luck, karma, life lessons. Those things seem to play a bigger role in fame.

The other big lesson I learned came from Jeff. As I mentioned, after the shows the cast would do improvisation, like the show *Who's Line Is It Anyway?*, only a gazillion times better. This one night, the audience got to ask questions. When one guy asked, "How do you make what you do funny?" the cast got quiet, then looked at Jeff like, "Well?"

He said, "You don't try to make it funny, you either are or you're not. But if you're just trying to be funny, you look like a clown. Everything has a reason, everything has a point. Before you say something, always know the point. When we do what we do, it has a reason. We never just get up here and act goofy. We ask, what is our point to this story? The comedy comes from getting to that point. Without it, there is no comedy."

As simple as that was, it has stuck with me all these years. "What is the point?" When he said it, he didn't sound condescending. He sounded honest, he sounded like he wanted the audience to know that it mattered to him and the cast that what they did was thoughtful, not stupid. Even if they all wore rubbers on their heads, there was a point to it.

The more I thought about his answer, the more I thought about things in my life. What was the point of so-and-so in my life, why did I need this or that?

In conversation, I stopped to think of what I was saying—what was my point?

And in readings it was especially helpful. Why did this person get sick, why did they get well, what was the point of losing their boyfriend, what was the point of taking this trip? Everything we go through has a purpose, a point, a reason.

As a psychic, I know that everything that happens to us happens for a reason. Everything. I've seen it a million times.

You lose your job? Your guides have another one they want you to get. Feel separated from people, always have? Maybe you are! But maybe you are for a good reason. Maybe because you've felt separated from people your whole life you aren't bound by the same fears that stop people from reaching their goals. You might make a fool of yourself. You might fail. So what? You've felt like a failure your whole life!

I can't tell you how many times guides look, in wonder, at the stupidity of people.

The answers are right there. Look at what's happened around you and ask yourself why things happened to you the way they did.

Trusting Intuition

My friend Marlene is one of those people I've known since I started out long ago. I would describe Marlene as a cross between a hooker and Yoda. She could be edgy and cold, but wise and understanding. Even back then I could tell she had been through a lot. She was very attractive, but in a hard way. She was about fifteen years older than I am, and because I looked younger than my years she always called me kid.

The first time I did a reading for her was at a restaurant. She had been referred to me by one of her friends, who described her to me as "larger than life." When she walked into the restaurant, I recognized her immediately. Big hair, big boobs, attractive face, smoking a tiparillo cigar. She was met by the manager, who told her they didn't allow cigars in the restaurant. "Sure, sure," she said as she ignored the manager and looked for me. Only after she spotted me waving did she acknowledge the manager and assure him she would put it out. She came over to the table and put out her hand to shake mine.

"So you're the psychic wonder boy I've been hearing about?" she asked. She shook my hand and sat down.

"Yup, that's me," I responded and I asked if she was the wild and crazy Marlene I had heard about. She studied my face and cackled. Just then the waitress came over and asked us if we wanted anything to drink. She pointed out once again that they didn't allow cigars in the restaurant. "Oh," she said, "I talked to the manager and he said it was okay. I'll take a Coke." Surprised, the waitress paused and then asked me. I asked for a Coke also, and the waitress left the table.

"Look kid, I only got a few minutes before they kick me out, so I just want to ask you a couple of questions, okay?"

"Ask away," I said.

"This guy I'm seeing, Harold, is he cheating on me?"

I smiled. Even at that age, I knew that was a bad question to ask. If he was, she probably wouldn't leave anyway. If confronted, her boyfriend would point out that the information came from a stupid psychic, and why would you believe a psychic over him? And if he wasn't, she wouldn't believe me because I might be wrong.

I noticed the waitress having a chat with the manager and pointing in our direction, so I knew I had to get to the point. "Yes," I said, "he is," and watched her take a deep draw off her cigar.

"That bastard," she said quietly, as she blew out the smoke. Now the ladies next to us were coughing. Marlene was oblivious.

The manager came to our table and asked Marlene once again to put out her cigar or leave. Ignoring the manager, Marlene asked me if it was a woman named Debbie. I looked at the manager, then to her. "Yeah," I said, "that feels about right."

The manager, now animated, asked Marlene if he heard him. Just then, the waitress came back with our drinks. Without acknowledging the manager, Marlene took one more puff from her cigar, stood up, blew it out angrily, and put it out in her Coke. "I fucking knew it," she said, and threw a five dollar bill on the table. "Thanks kid." And with that, she was gone.

That was my introduction to Marlene. I liked her immediately.

I saw Marlene a lot over the years. Sometimes she would disappear for a year or two, but she always came back, like the swallows of Capistrano. Each time she came back, she had a new adventure to talk about, a new romance, an exotic city. And when we talked it wasn't like a typical reading, it was more to confirm what she was already feeling. She trusted her intuition 95 percent of the time, but that last 5 percent, she was iffy. For me, she was the easiest person I've ever given a reading to.

If she had a feeling to go someplace, she would go. If she felt she needed to do something, she would do it, most of the time.

Each time she came, like all of us, she was getting older. Something about her fast life seemed to age her quicker than most. Then one day her daughter showed up. I stood at the door, uncertain what to say, and I heard this growly voice say, "Kid, it's me, Marlene."

She had gotten a face lift and she looked twenty years younger.

She never minced words or beat around the bush. If she disagreed with what I said, she'd tell me it was bullshit, but then pat me on my knee and cackle at my reaction. She wasn't much of a hugger, which was fine because she smoked like a chimney. I always tried to stay downwind.

The last time Marlene came for a reading, she was happy. Smoking and age had taken a toll on her face and teeth, but she wasn't concerned. I asked her if she was going to get another face lift, but she replied that one was enough. Besides, she said, she knew it was the smoking and she loved her smoking. She had been told to quit a long time ago, but it was her contention that they couldn't always tell her what to do. "I don't always listen to my intuition," she said.

She came to ask me what was next. This was unusual for her, because like I said, normally she would ask for confirmation on what she already knew. But she said she wasn't getting anything anymore.

When I sat down to figure it out, my heart sank. I got that feeling, when I know a person's time is almost up. She could tell by my expression that I was struggling for the words to say. She changed the subject. "Do you ever get tired of telling people things they already know?" she asked.

"Yeah," I replied, "I do."

"Maybe you should write another book, but this time, point that out."

"Jesus," I said. "With my ADD I barely made it through the last book."

She smiled. "Hey kid, I'm going to go," she said as she got up. I was relieved, but also sad. We both knew what was going on, but neither of us wanted to talk about it. As she got to the door, she paused. "Will it hurt?" she asked.

"Writing another book? Fuck yeah, it's going to hurt," I joked.

I saw her looking in my eyes. "No," I said, "it won't."

She reached out her arms and hugged me. "I love you kid," she said and walked out the door.

Marlene passed six months later in her sleep.

I don't know that I would have written this book if Marlene didn't come that day, though maybe I would have. But she lived her life believing her guides and trusting that everything happens for a reason. The least I can do is do the same.

To Write the Author

If you wish to contact the author or would like more information about this book, please write to the author in care of Llewellyn Worldwide, and we will forward your request. Both the author and the publisher appreciate hearing from you and learning of your enjoyment of this book and how it has helped you. Llewellyn Worldwide cannot guarantee that every letter written to the author can be answered, but all will be forwarded. Please write to:

Michael Bodine
℅ Llewellyn Worldwide
2143 Wooddale Drive
Woodbury, MN 55125-2989

Please enclose a self-addressed stamped envelope for reply, or $1.00 to cover costs. If outside the USA, enclose an international postal reply coupon.

GET MORE AT **LLEWELLYN.COM**

Visit us online to browse hundreds of our books and decks, plus sign up to receive our e-newsletters and exclusive online offers.

- **Free tarot readings • Spell-a-Day • Moon phases**
- **Recipes, spells, and tips • Blogs • Encyclopedia**
- **Author interviews, articles, and upcoming events**

GET SOCIAL WITH **LLEWELLYN**

Find us on   🐦 **@LlewellynBooks**

www.Facebook.com/LlewellynBooks

GET BOOKS AT **LLEWELLYN**

LLEWELLYN ORDERING INFORMATION

 Order online: Visit our website at www.llewellyn.com to select your books and place an order on our secure server.

Order by phone:
- Call toll free within the US at 1-877-NEW-WRLD (1-877-639-9753)
- We accept VISA, MasterCard, American Express, and Discover.
- Canadian customers must use credit cards.

Order by mail:
Send the full price of your order (MN residents add 6.875% sales tax) in US funds plus postage and handling to: Llewellyn Worldwide, 2143 Wooddale Drive, Woodbury, MN 55125-2989

POSTAGE AND HANDLING

STANDARD (US):
(Please allow 12 business days)
$30.00 and under, add $6.00.
$30.01 and over, FREE SHIPPING.

INTERNATIONAL ORDERS,
INCLUDING CANADA:
$16.00 for one book, plus $3.00 for each additional book.

Visit us online for more shipping options.
Prices subject to change.

FREE CATALOG!

To order, call
1-877-
NEW-WRLD
ext. 8236
or visit our
website

Comforting Messages & Lessons from Loved Ones in Spirit

Journey to the *Afterlife*

KRISTY ROBINETT

Author of *It's a Wonderful Afterlife*

Journey to the Afterlife
Comforting Messages & Lessons from Loved Ones in Spirit
KRISTY ROBINETT

Journey to the Afterlife reveals the true nature of heaven, hell, and the in-between from spirits who are there. Join Kristy Robinett as she shares soul-stirring messages from her many years of practice as a professional psychic medium. This book answers the most persistent questions about the afterlife, showing what kinds of lessons are learned as spirits evolve and grow in light and peace. Have you ever wondered what heaven is like? Or how a child's experience of the afterlife is different than an adult's? Is there such a thing as hell or purgatory?

With dozens of moving case studies and remarkable examples, *Journey to the Afterlife* shows how our loved ones are given the opportunity to grow and find happiness on the other side. These messages are a great comfort to Kristy's clients, and they will touch your heart while helping you move forward on your own personal journey.

978-0-7387-5269-3, 264 pp., 5 ¼ x 8   **$16.99**

A
Survival Guide
for those who have
PSYCHIC ABILITIES
············· AND ···············
DON'T KNOW WHAT TO DO WITH THEM

Lisa Anne Rooney

A Survival Guide for Those Who Have Psychic Abilities and Don't Know What to Do With Them

LISA ANNE ROONEY

For many people, natural psychic abilities are more disruptive than they are helpful, and sometimes they're downright terrifying. This empowering book shares tips and techniques for learning to use your psychic abilities in a way that enhances your life and helps you balance your mind, body, and spirit.

Discover how to tell the difference between spirits and ghosts. Learn how to work with negative entities and protect yourself from psychic harm. Explore how to receive messages and channel the wisdom of your guides. Lisa Anne Rooney provides crucial advice on everything from energy clearing to taking spiritual lessons to heart. She also offers inspiring insights and words of encouragement for those times when you need it most.

978-0-7387-5651-6, 216 pp., 5 ¼ x 8   **$16.99**

To order, call 1-877-NEW-WRLD
Prices subject to change without notice
Order at Llewellyn.com 24 hours a day, 7 days a week!

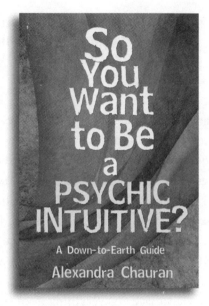

So
You
Want
to Be
a
PSYCHIC
INTUITIVE?

A Down-to-Earth Guide

Alexandra Chauran

So You Want to be a Psychic Intuitive?

ALEXANDRA CHAURAN

Dependable guidance, communication with departed loved ones, helping friends and family—the lifelong rewards of a strong psychic connection are countless. Whether you're a beginner or already in touch with your intuition, this encouraging, conversational, and hands-on guide can help you improve psychic abilities. Featuring illustrative anecdotes and easy exercises, you'll learn how to achieve a receptive state, identify your source of information, receive messages, and interpret coincidences, dreams, and symbols. Step-by-step instructions make it easy to try a variety of psychic techniques and divination, such as telepathy, channeling, spirit communication, automatic writing, and scrying. There's also practical advice for wisely applying your enhanced psychic skills personally and professionally.

978-0-7387-3065-3, 264 pp., 5 ¼ x 8   **$14.95**
